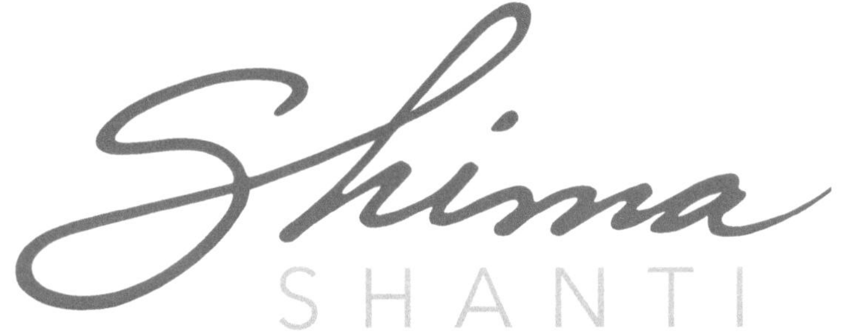

encaustic fine artist

2022

ISBN: 978-0-9915481-5-6

Publishing Consultant, Project Manager
and Book Interior Layout and Cover Design by
Karen Saunders, www.KarenSaundersAssoc.com.

Original Art Photo-Images by Jim Kelly.

Photography by Celia Young, www.DesignedImages.com

Published by
Peace Waters
San Diego, CA 92128
www.ShimaShanti.com

WEBSTER'S DEFINITION

encaustic noun

en·caus·tic | in-ˈkȯ-stik

Definition of *encaustic*

: a paint made from pigment mixed with melted beeswax and resin and after application fused by heat. A work of art produced by this method is called encaustic. The word encaustic – meaning to burn in – originates from the Latin word encausticus and from Greek enkaustikos.

"Webster said nothing of how it can transcend the artist into an existential world of natural beauty and transport the beholder into etheric wonder by its simple ingredients."

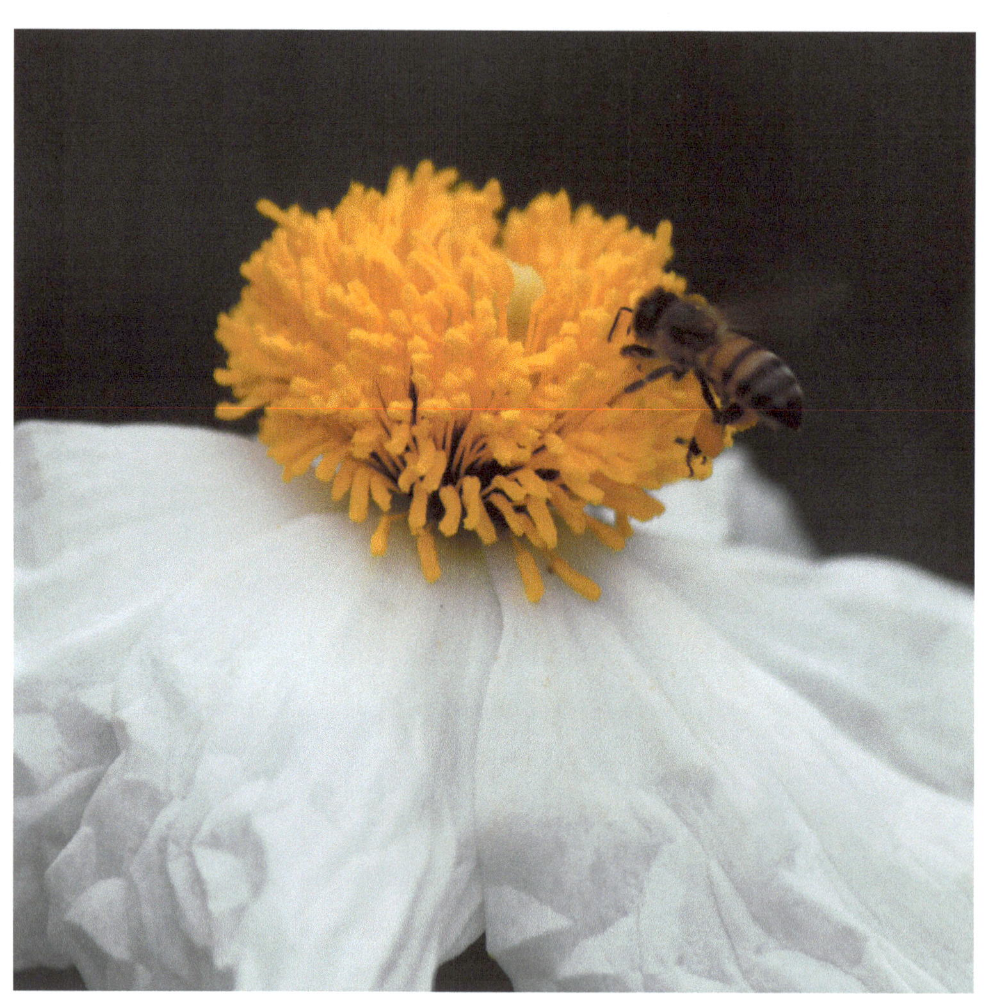

"Nothing in the definition of encaustic

describes the lucscious fragrance of grasses and wildflowers

radiating from melting pots of wax straight from the honey and the hive;

Or the transparency, translucency, and luminosity of this

alchemical elixir of wax and pigment."

CONTENTS

COLLECTIONS

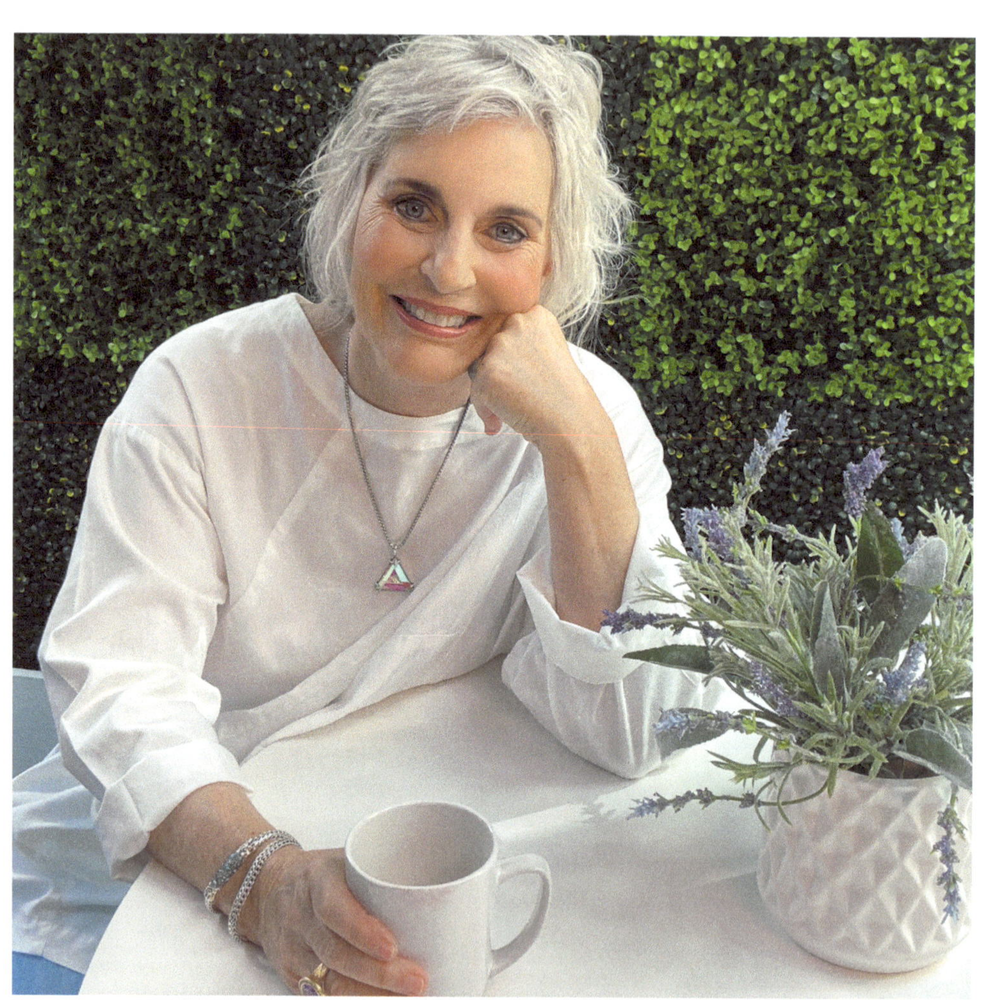

ARTIST STATEMENT

What lies beyond what appears to be and the quest for the true meaning of life inspire Shima Shanti.

Shima is a beeswax and fire painter in the ancient art form of encaustic. The flow and fusion of molten beeswax in her abstract impressionistic paintings convey the mystical harmony and infinite beauty of our natural world.

Grounded by the horizon – with wax, fire, and brush in hand – she is free to explore Spirit within the physical realm. At some point the horizon blurs and boundaries dissolve. The painting reveals its message.

Shima holds a special reverence for the *unseen* details in the complex and labor-intensive encaustic process. The energy she infuses into each painting stirs something within us, awakens us, and beckons us to linger a moment longer in a shared experience with the Artist. This is the gift; the gift of her art.

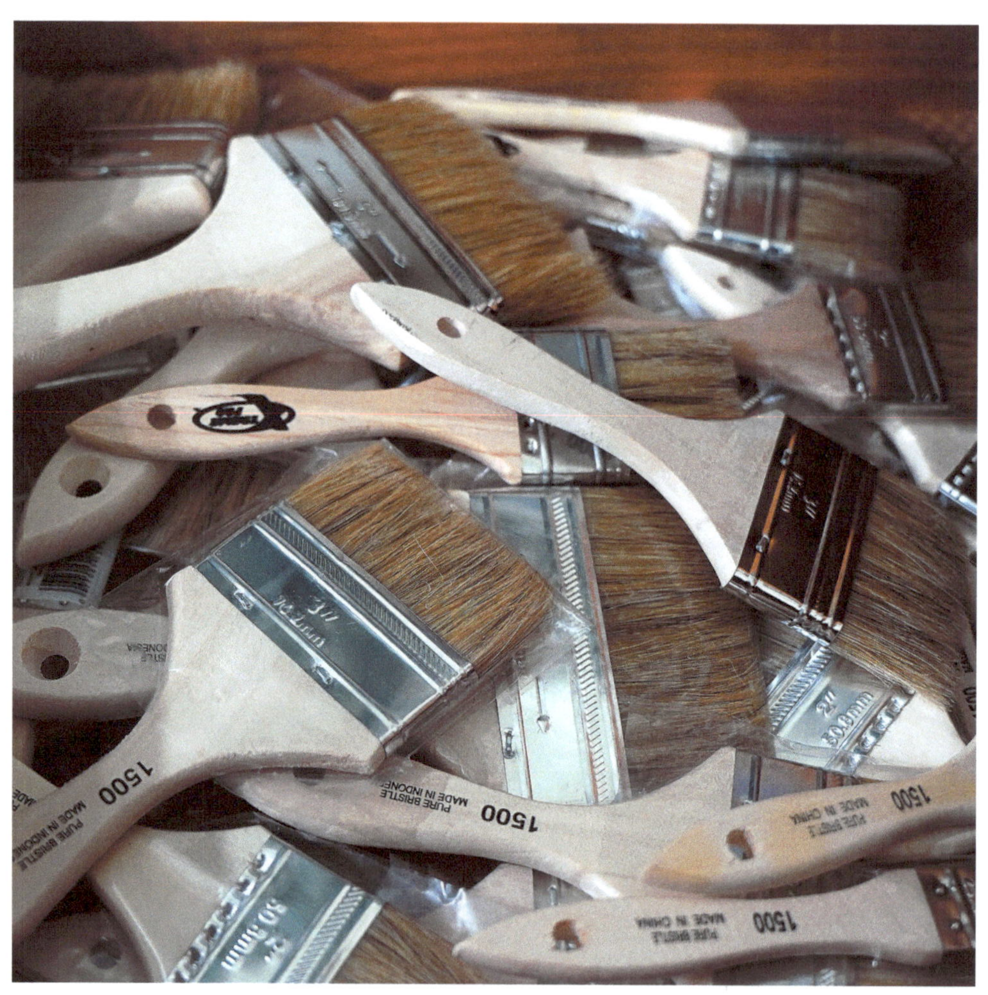
1500
PURE BRISTLE
MADE IN CHINA
1500
1500
PURE BRISTLE
MADE IN CHINA
1500

WHAT IS ENCAUSTIC?

ENCAUSTIC'S EVOLUTION

Painting with wax is one of the world's oldest art forms. Encaustic art can be traced back to Ancient Greece, where seafarers protected and adorned their ships and Grecian artists painted and sculpted with pigmented wax.

After the conquest of Alexander in 330 BC many Grecians migrated to Egypt bringing with them their art and culture. After the death of Cleopatra in 30 BC, Roman citizenry followed. The fusion of these three great civilizations, and their artistic, cultural and ethnic influence is evidenced in the Egyptian Fayum portraits. These 2,000 year-old encaustic artworks painted on wood mummy cases in the Greek style and Roman design, are still today, remarkably preserved.

Now, there is a resurgence of enthusiasm and interest in this ancient, natural and organic medium. For artist and viewer, Encaustic art responds to our quest: To balance our high-tech society with a connection to the natural world; to cherish and preserve an ancient art form, and to create significant and lasting contemporary art in homage to the artists who came before.

THE PROCESS

The complex and labor-intensive method of painting with beeswax and fire follows a similar process. Melt beeswax mixed with earth pigments and a natural tree resin called Damar. Paint and lightly fuse with the flame of a torch. Repeat. There can be up to 50+ layers of beeswax in every encaustic painting. Each layer of wax is fused into the layer beneath it. The encaustic surface can be smoothed and polished to a high gloss or left textured; rough yet refined. It can be cast and sculpted, combined with oil and pastel, or left in its natural hue. There are no limits to the freedom and expression of encaustic painting.

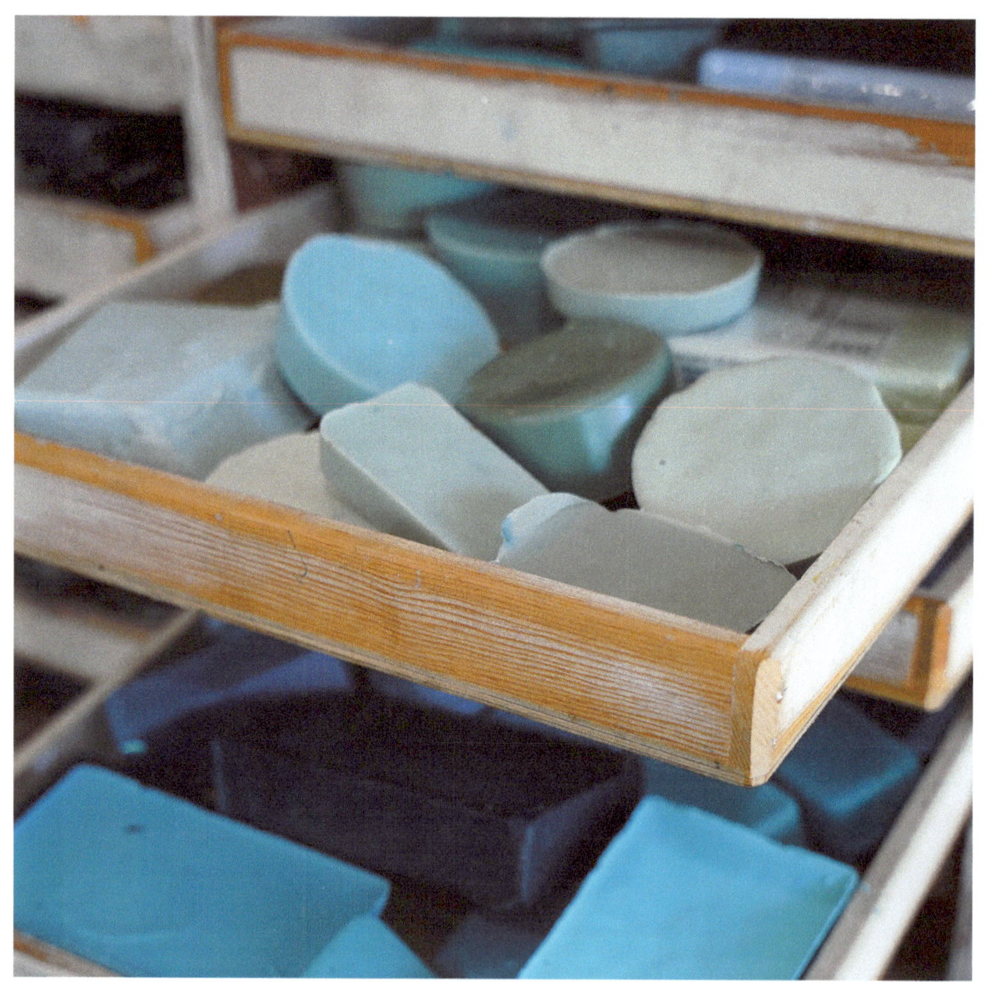

CARE

Like all fine art paintings, encaustic art is durable, archival, and created to last; however, it requires common-sense care to protect and preserve its beauty.

Beeswax is one of nature's best preservatives. It is impervious to moisture and will not yellow or darken with time. However, it is sensitive to extreme heat and cold and is best kept at normal room temperatures.

A small amount of the natural tree resin called Damar is added to the beeswax making it a very durable paint medium. Damar raises the melting temperature and increases the hardness of the beeswax. It is unlikely your painting will ever melt, nevertheless, it is best to avoid direct sunlight and extreme temperatures; and if handled roughly, it can be scratched, gouged, or chipped.

It is customary for encaustic artworks to be left unframed; however, a floating frame is a beautiful option to protect your painting while leaving the unique interest of the edges exposed. Encaustic art should not be framed under glass or acrylic which can damage the surface and conceal the translucent beauty of the many layers.

Encaustic art will completely cure within 12 months becoming ever clearer and more translucent. During the curing process, the artwork may appear cloudy or matte. This is a natural byproduct of the release of lipids in the wax called "bloom" and is not a defect. If your painting appears "dull" simply buff the cool surface in a circular motion with a soft, lint-free cotton cloth to restore its luster. After the painting is fully cured it will retain its natural high-gloss finish.

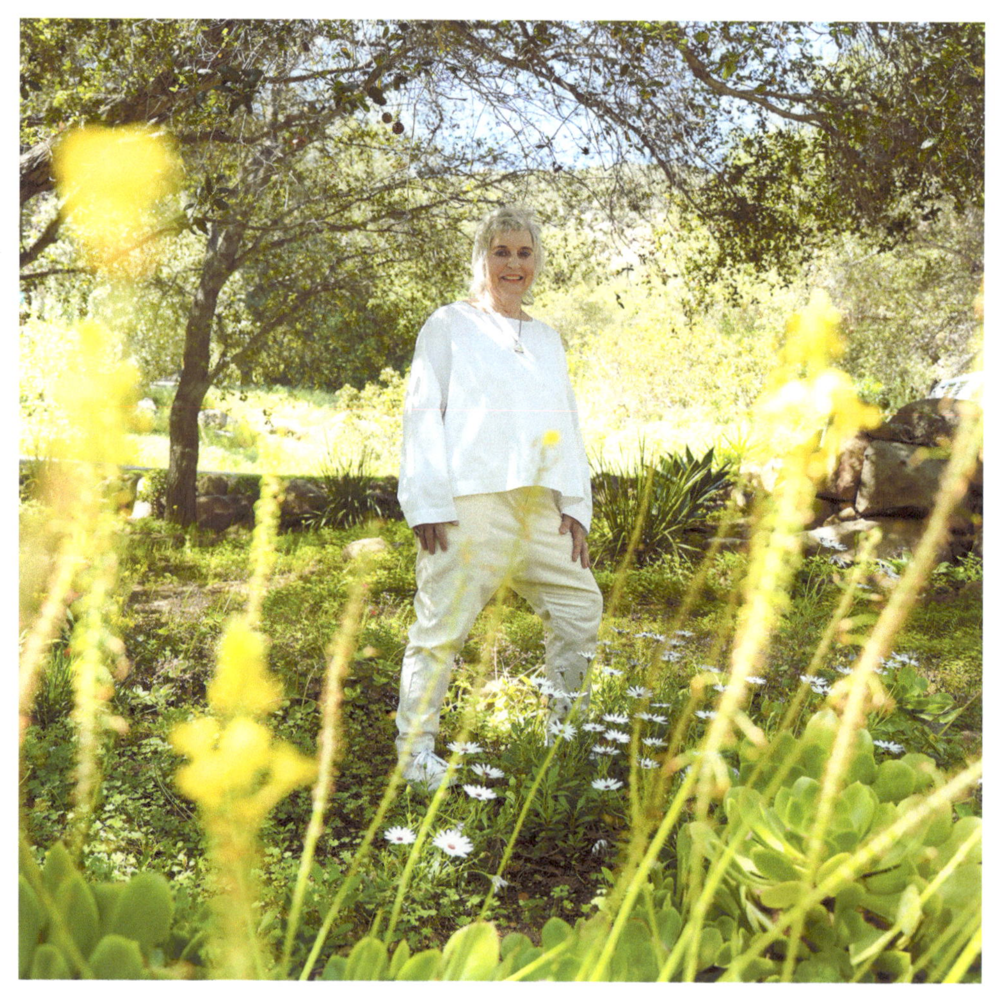

TO ME

Painting with beeswax connects me to nature and draws me into sacred resonance. It is my open-eye meditation. Similar to life, every layer of beeswax fused one upon the other represents moments in time creating life's journey. The dimensional depth of multi-layers of beeswax reveals an untold story left to our imagining.

COLLECTIONS

COLLECTION:

A CLEARING FOR SILENCE

The deep well of stillness.

The merging of all and nothing.

Clarity in the absence of detail.

"Encaustic art is my language.

I speak to those who listen with their heart.

Not everyone will understand what I am saying."

Absence of Thought

36 x 36 in

May 2021

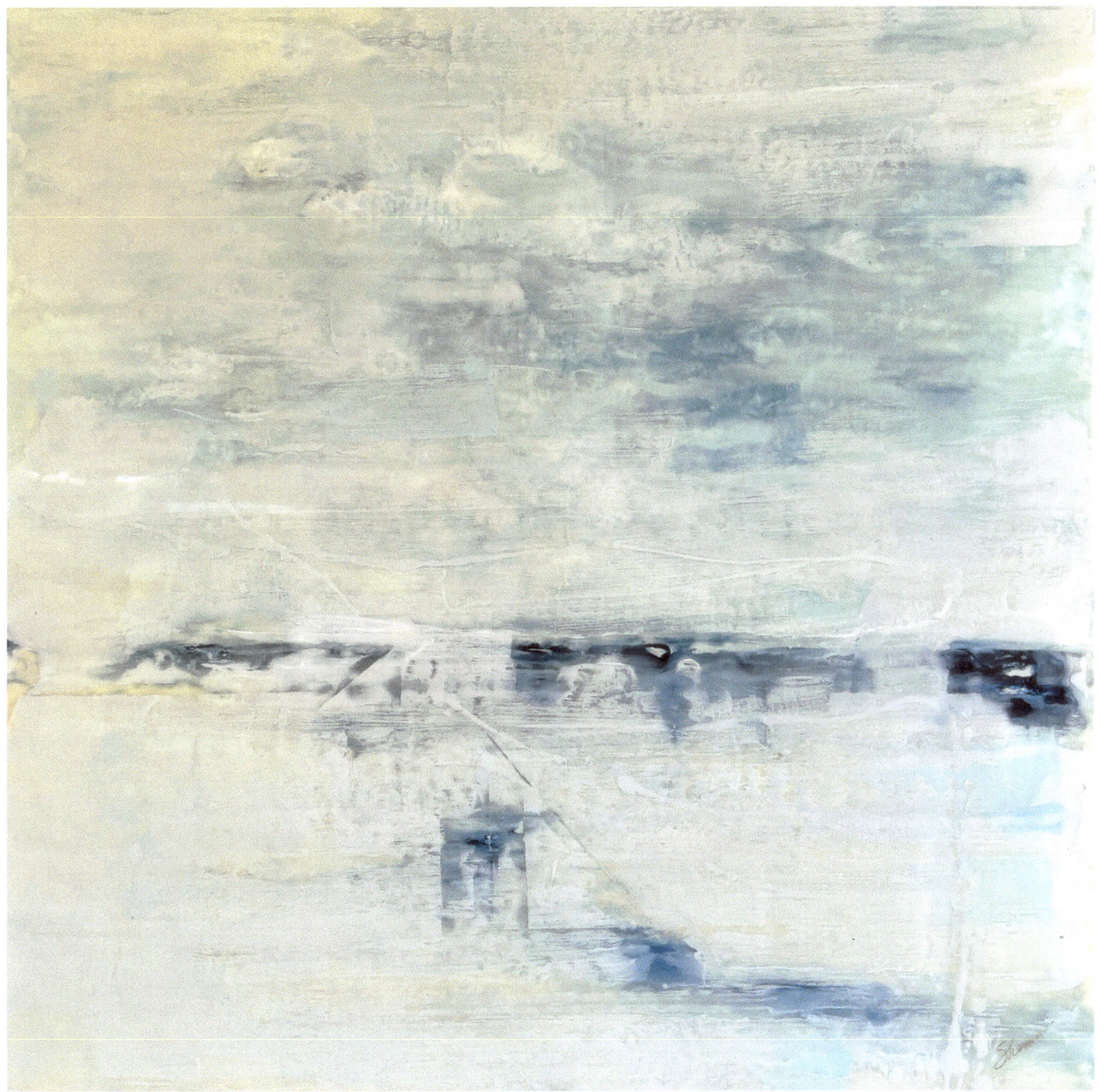

Another Time

36 x 36 in

May 2021

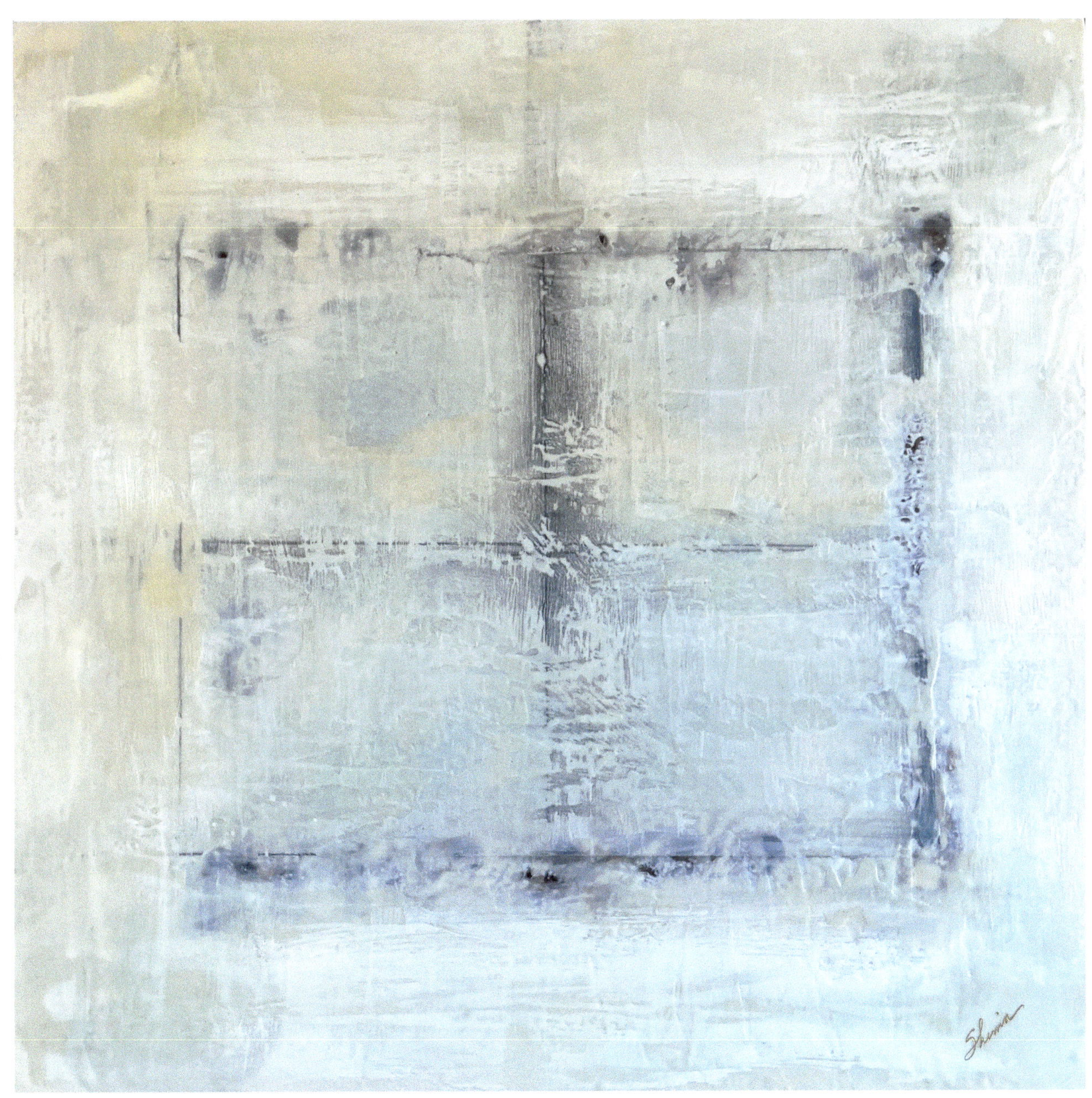

Pier View

36 x 36 in

June 2022

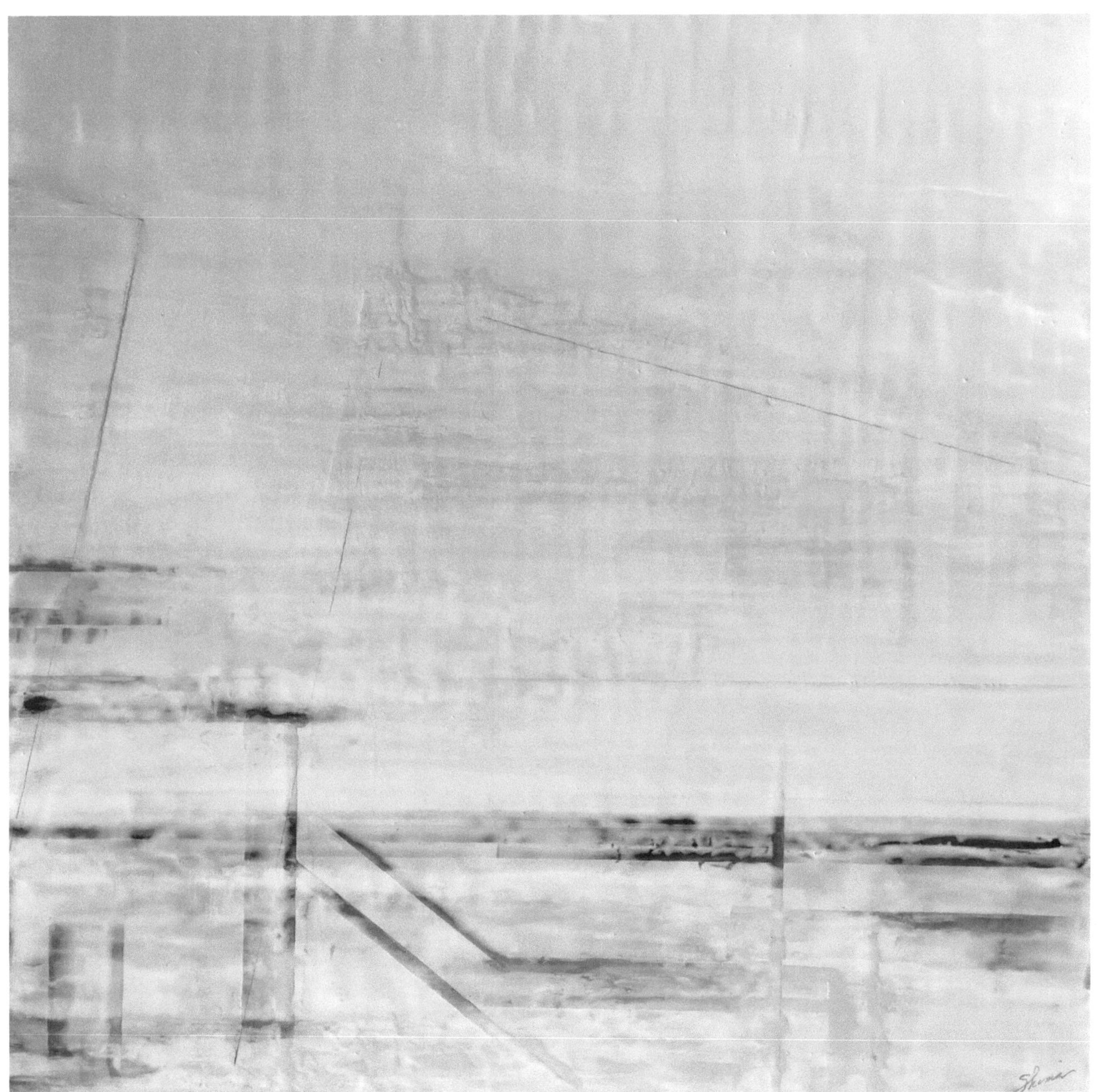

Sea Sway

36 x 36 in

May 2021

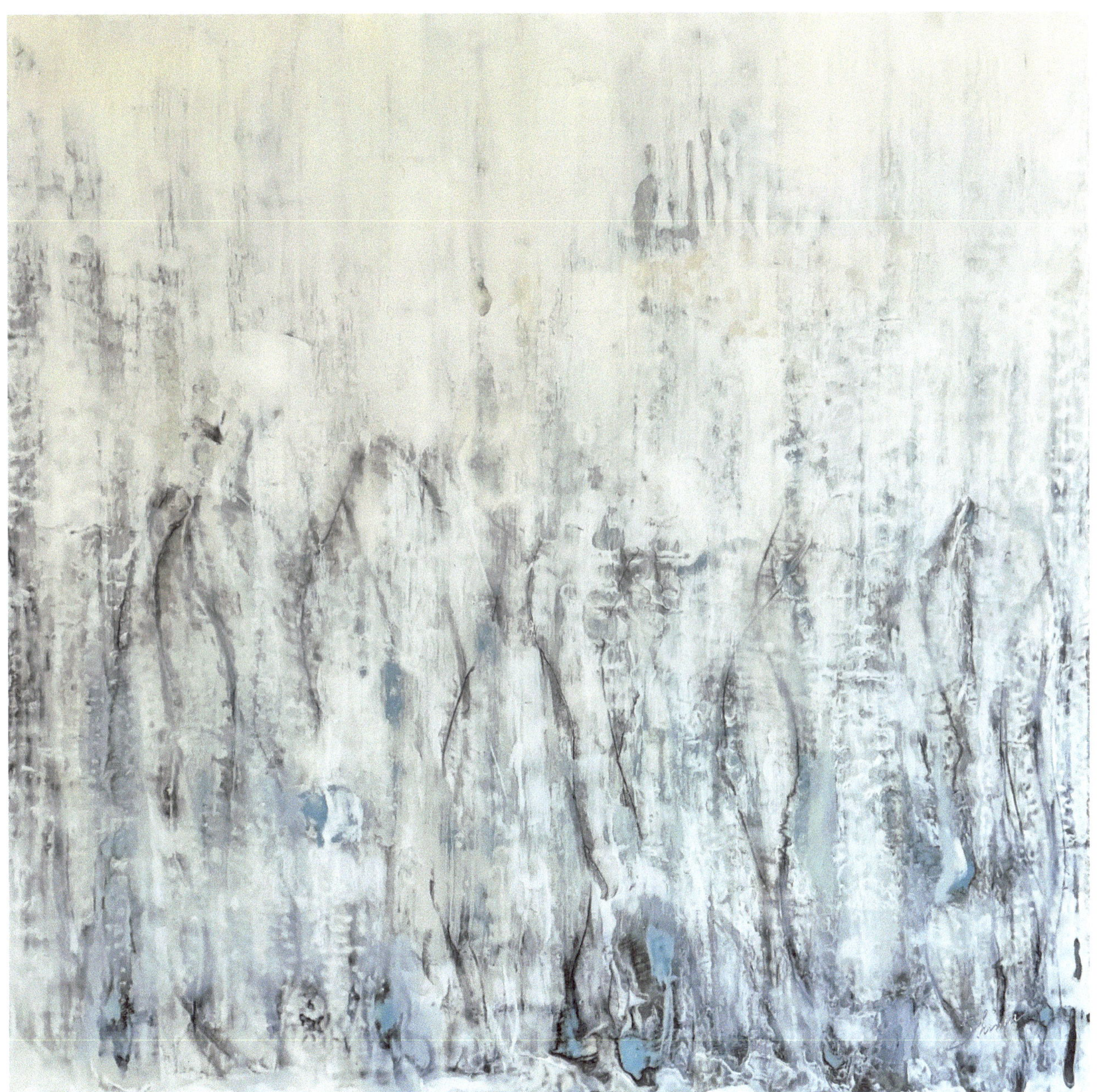

Silent Shadows I

36 x 36 in

May 2022

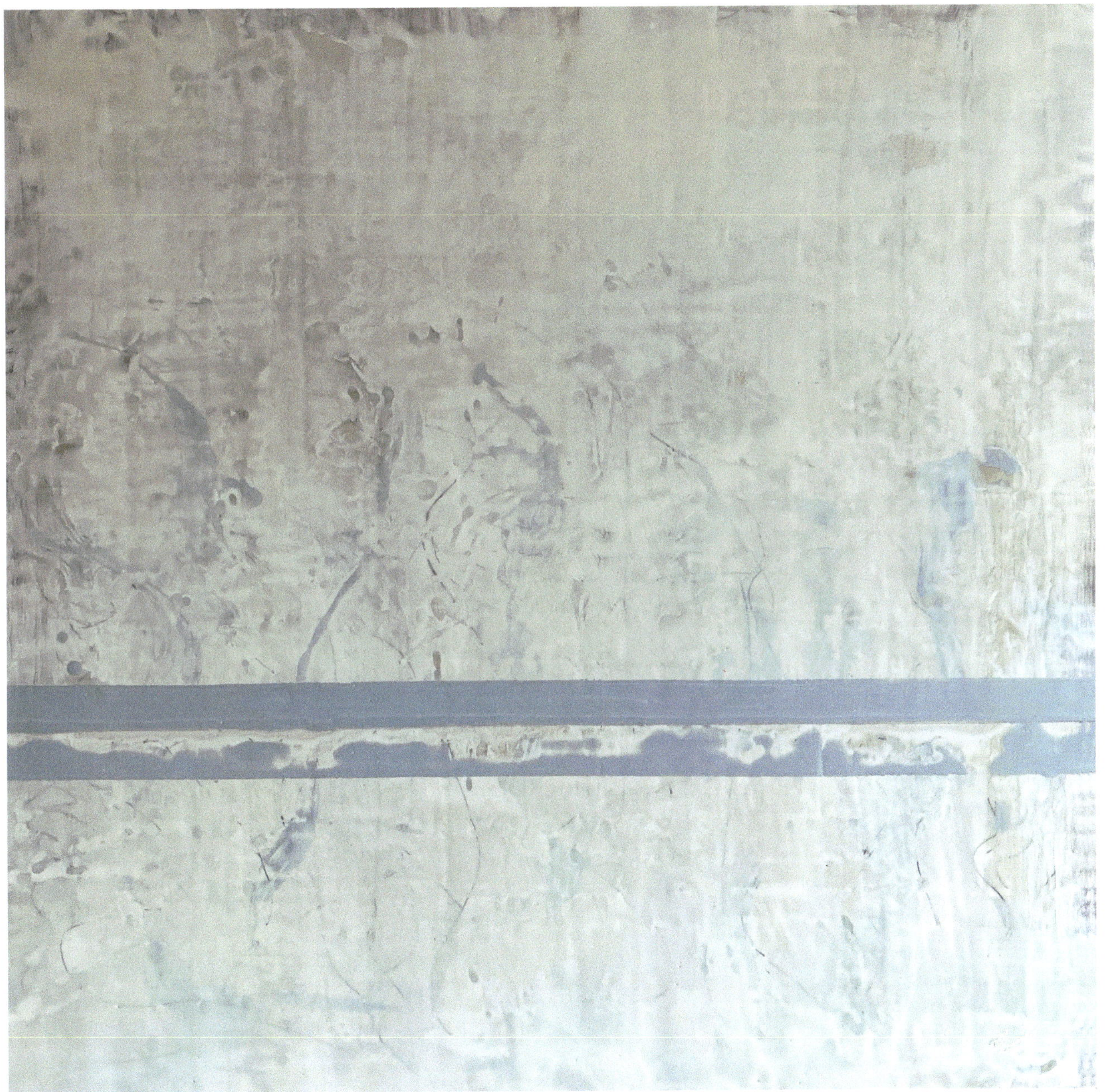

Wind Swept

36 x 36 in

February 2021

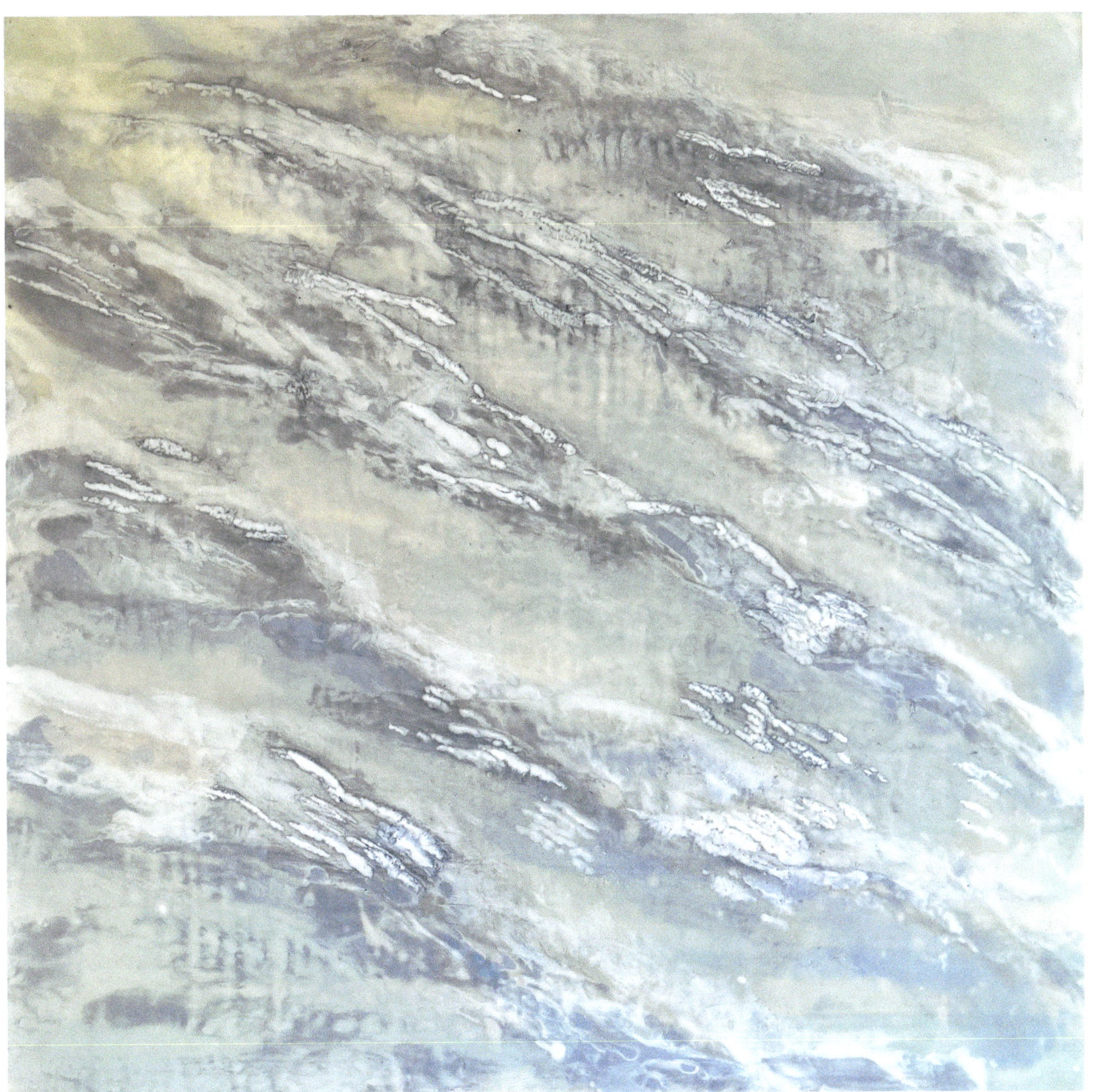

COLLECTION:

HIKARU

Japanese for Light and Radiance.

The stillness of silence.

The point of union when all colors combine into the absence of color.

White gilded in Gold.

"There comes a point when I am painting, when it is really good. Goose bump good. Don't touch it good! But, it is still not done and I know it. I am torn; if I keep going with the next pass of the torch, I can alter it irreversibly. I face a moment of uncertainty. I fire the torch. I take the next relevant step."

Cacophony

24 x 24 in

April 2020

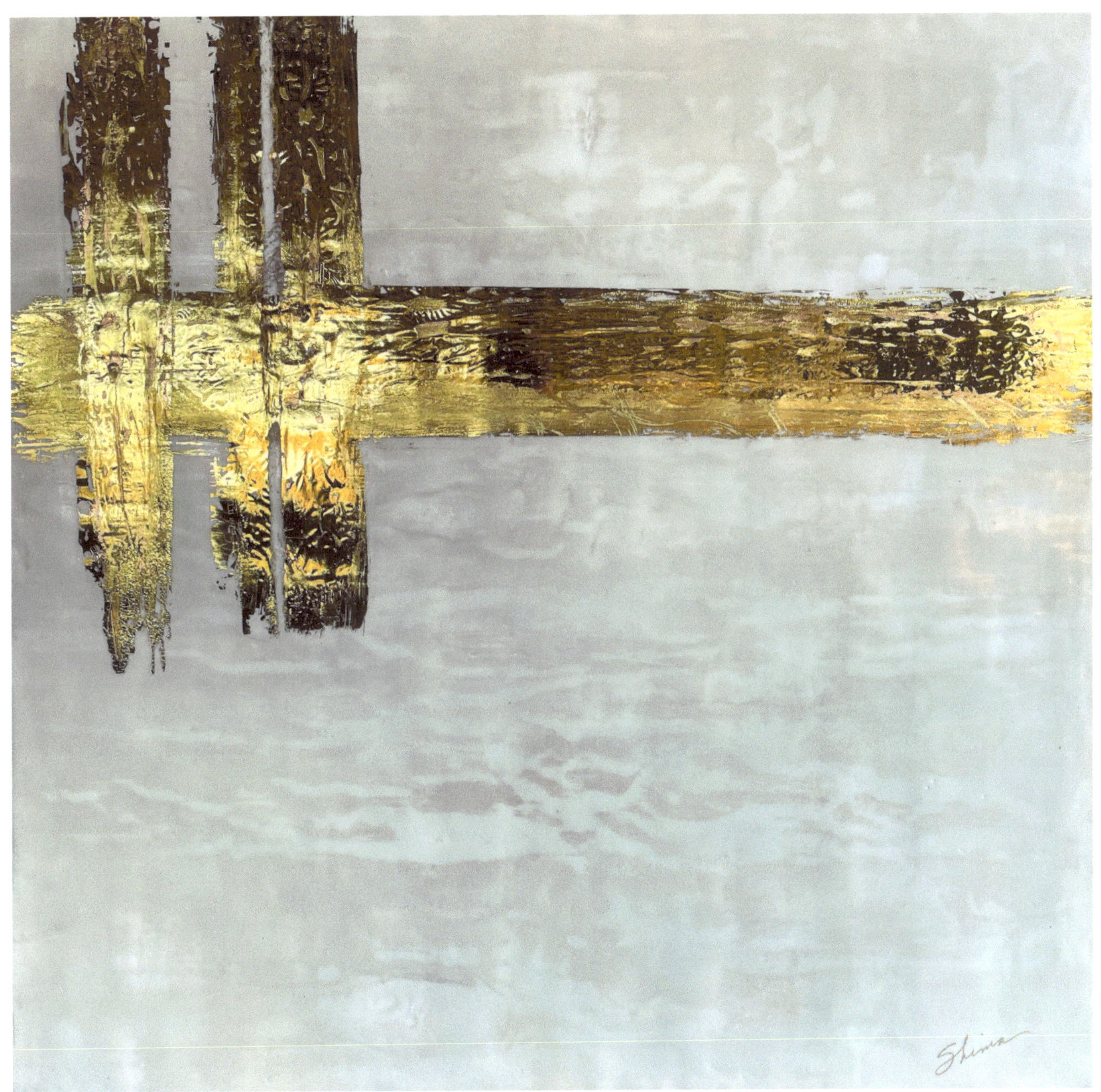

Ceaseless Prayer

36 x 36 x in

June 2020

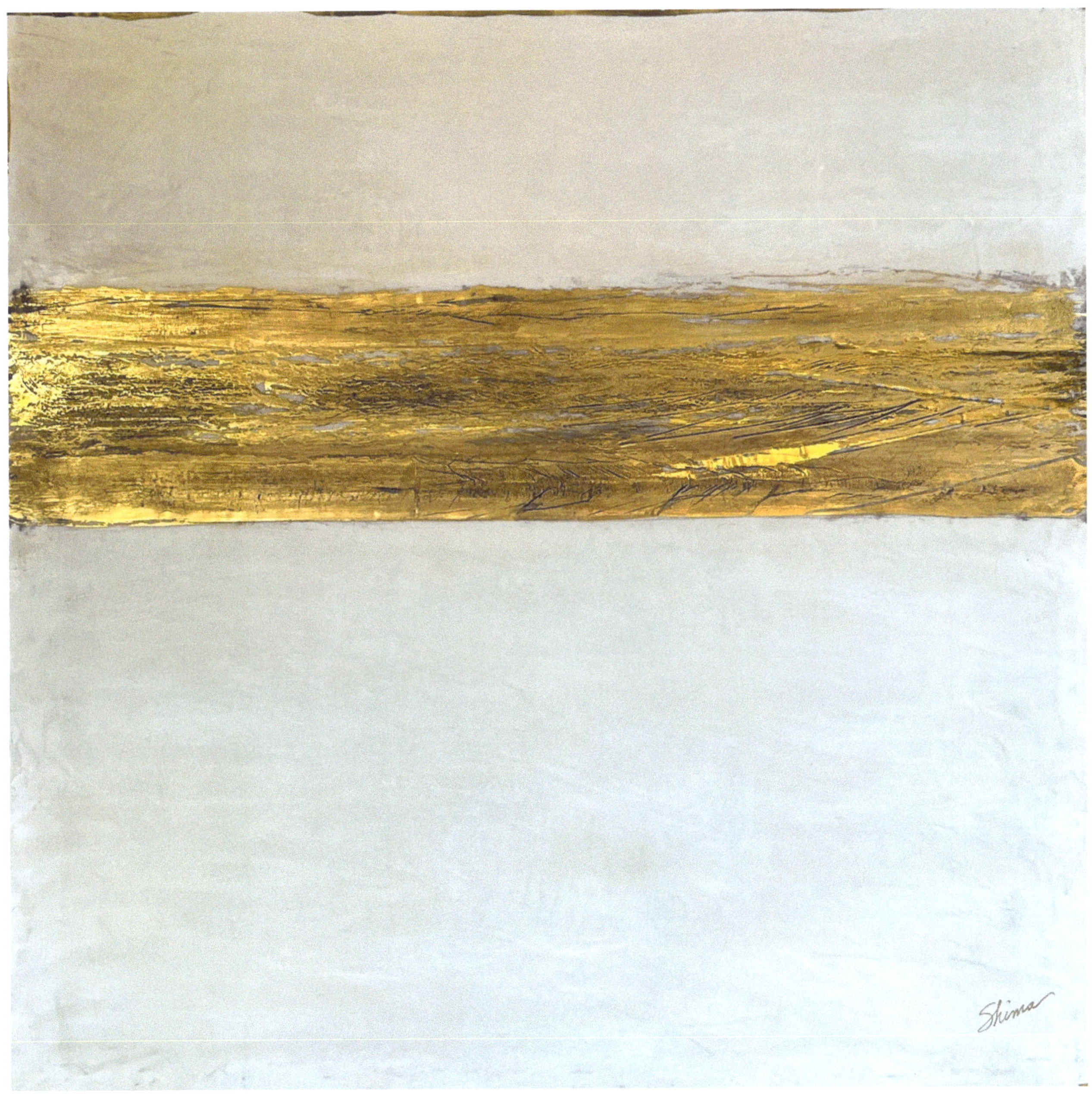
Shima

Choicepoint

36 x 36 in

January 2021

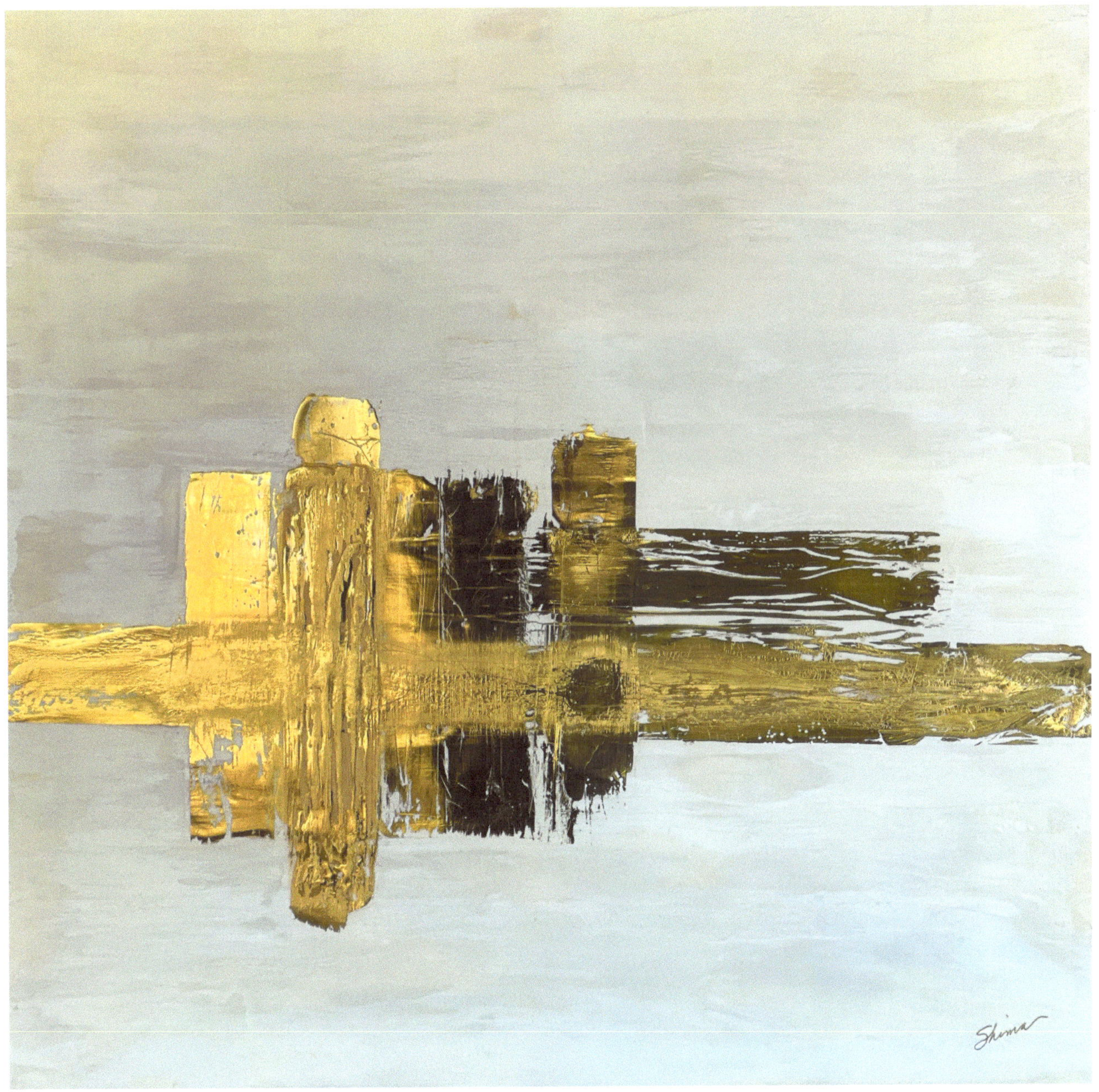
Shima

Guide Your Way On

36 x 36 in

May 2020

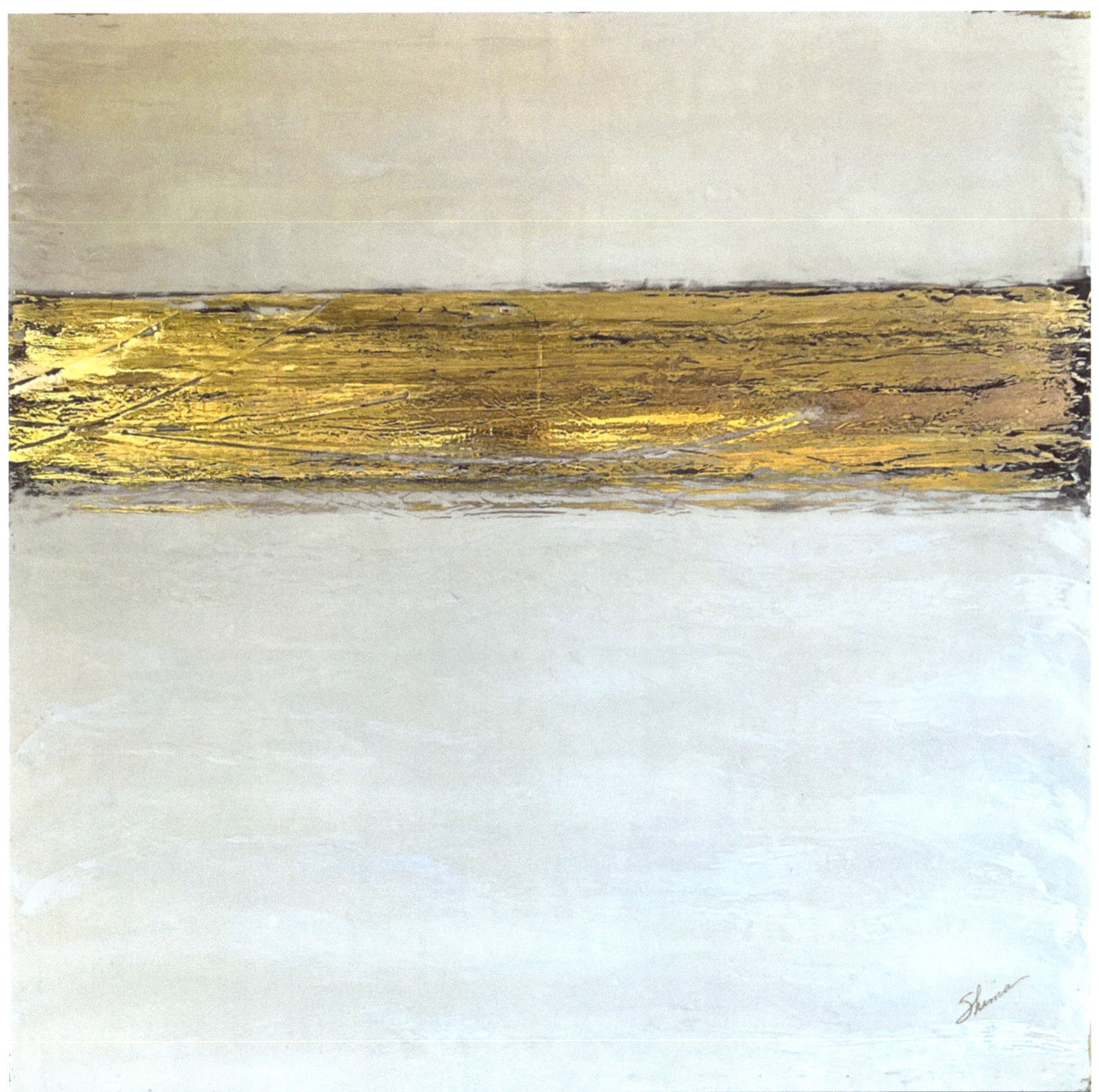

Innermost Dwelling

36 x 36 in

March 2021

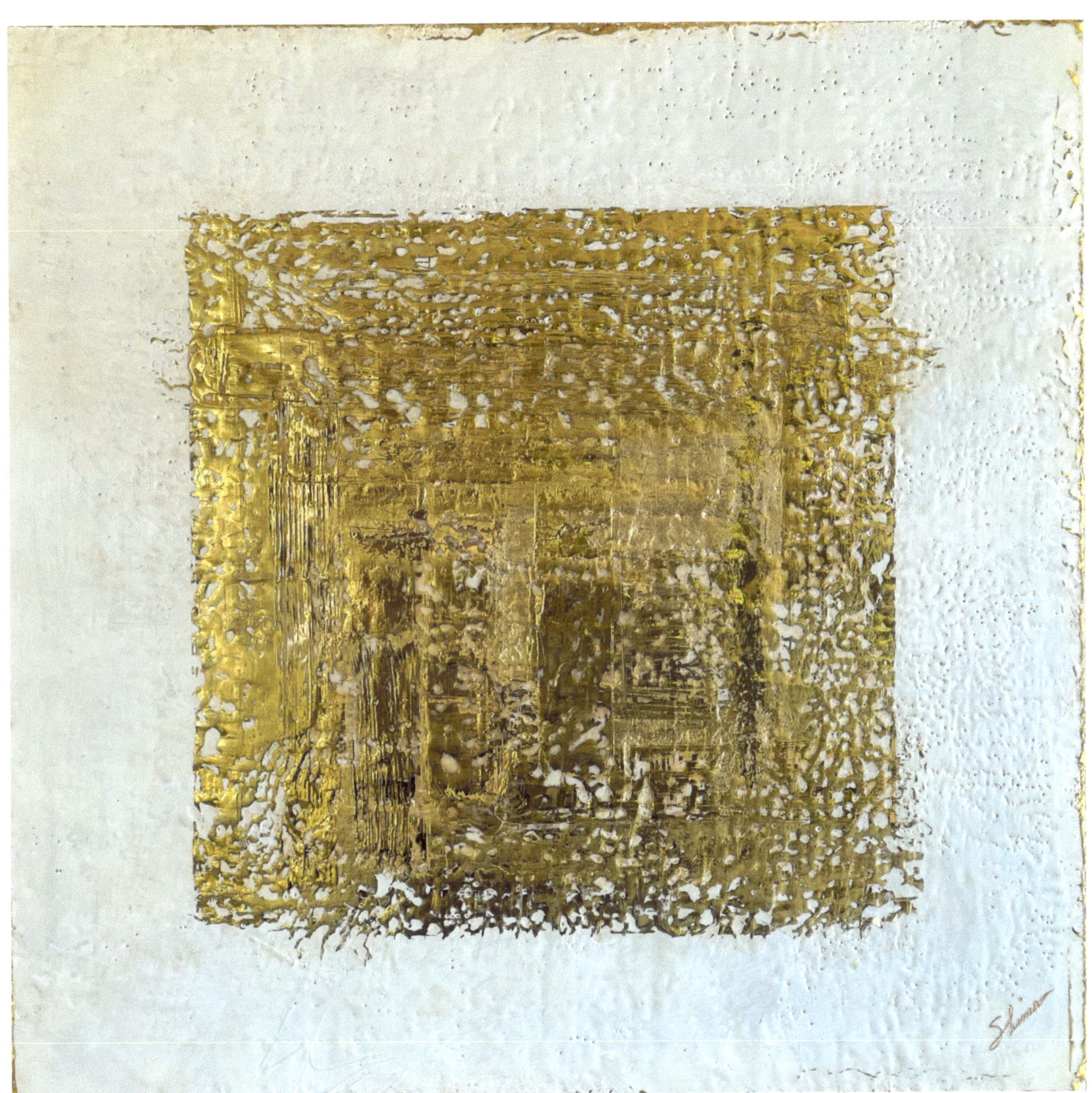

Intersect

36 x 36 in

May 2021

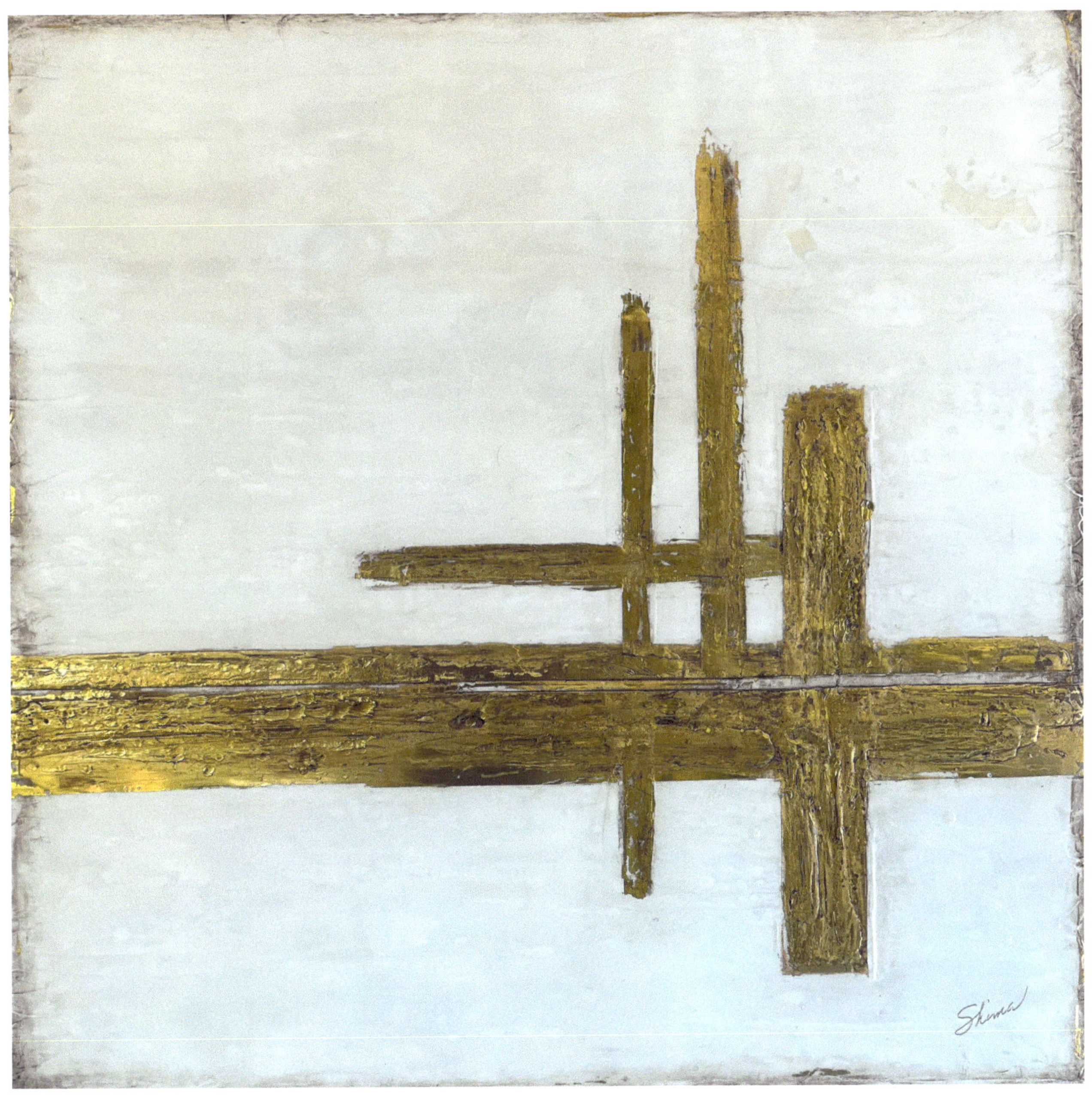

COLLECTION:

HOMAGE TO DIEBENKORN

Lines, angles and planes of color balanced on the horizon.

The invisible and underlying structure in nature.

Tension beneath a calm of peace.

Improbable space.

Seeing beyond what appears to be.

"Painting with encaustic is a series of choices.

Every brush stroke and pass of the torch calls for a choice.

Each decision overlays and intersects with another

defining the whole of the finished artwork.

In some paintings, the effect is immediate;

in others the meaning is concealed layers deep."

In All Its Many Forms

36 x 36 in

July 2022

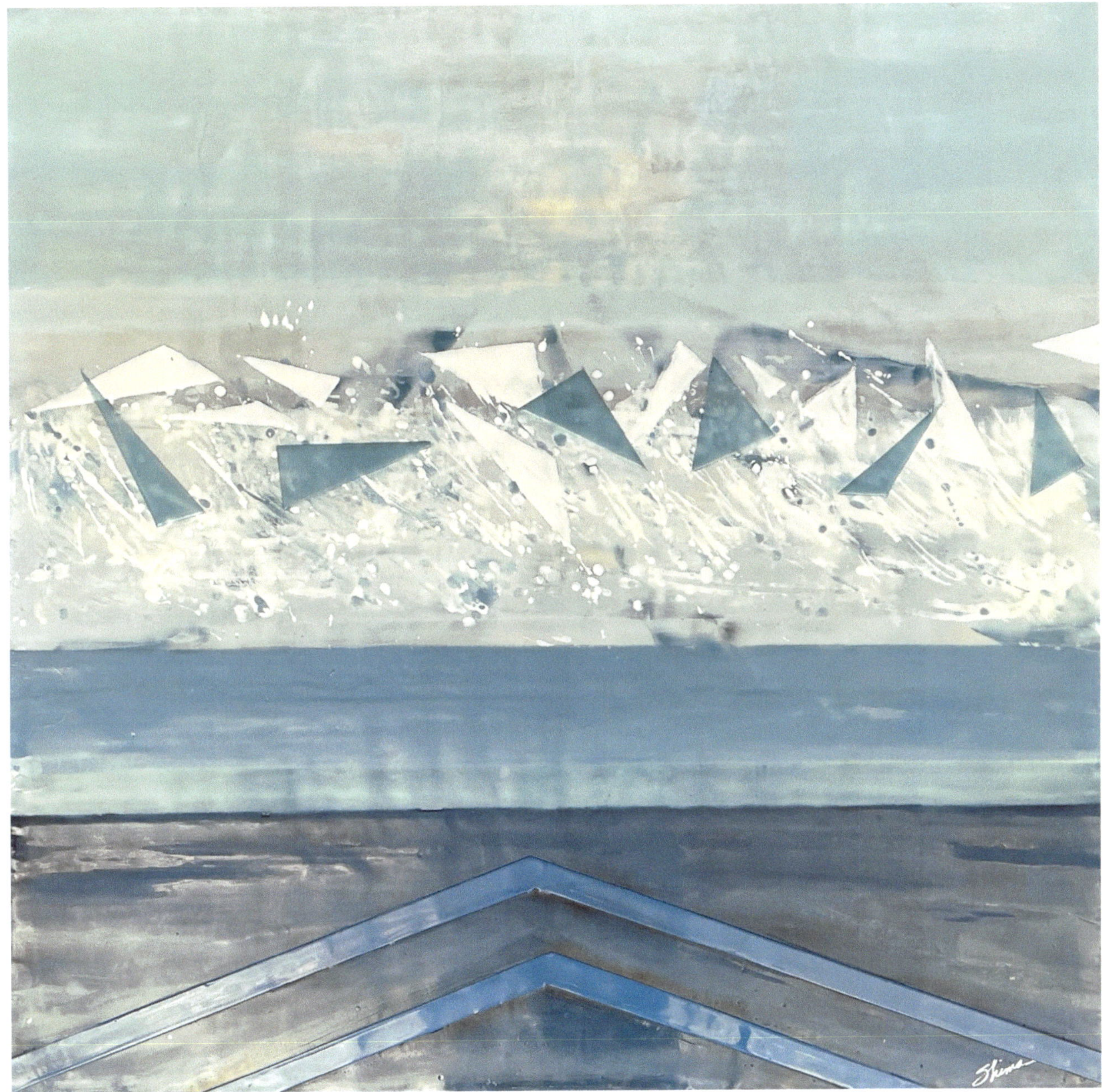

High Water Mark

36 x 36 in

May 2022

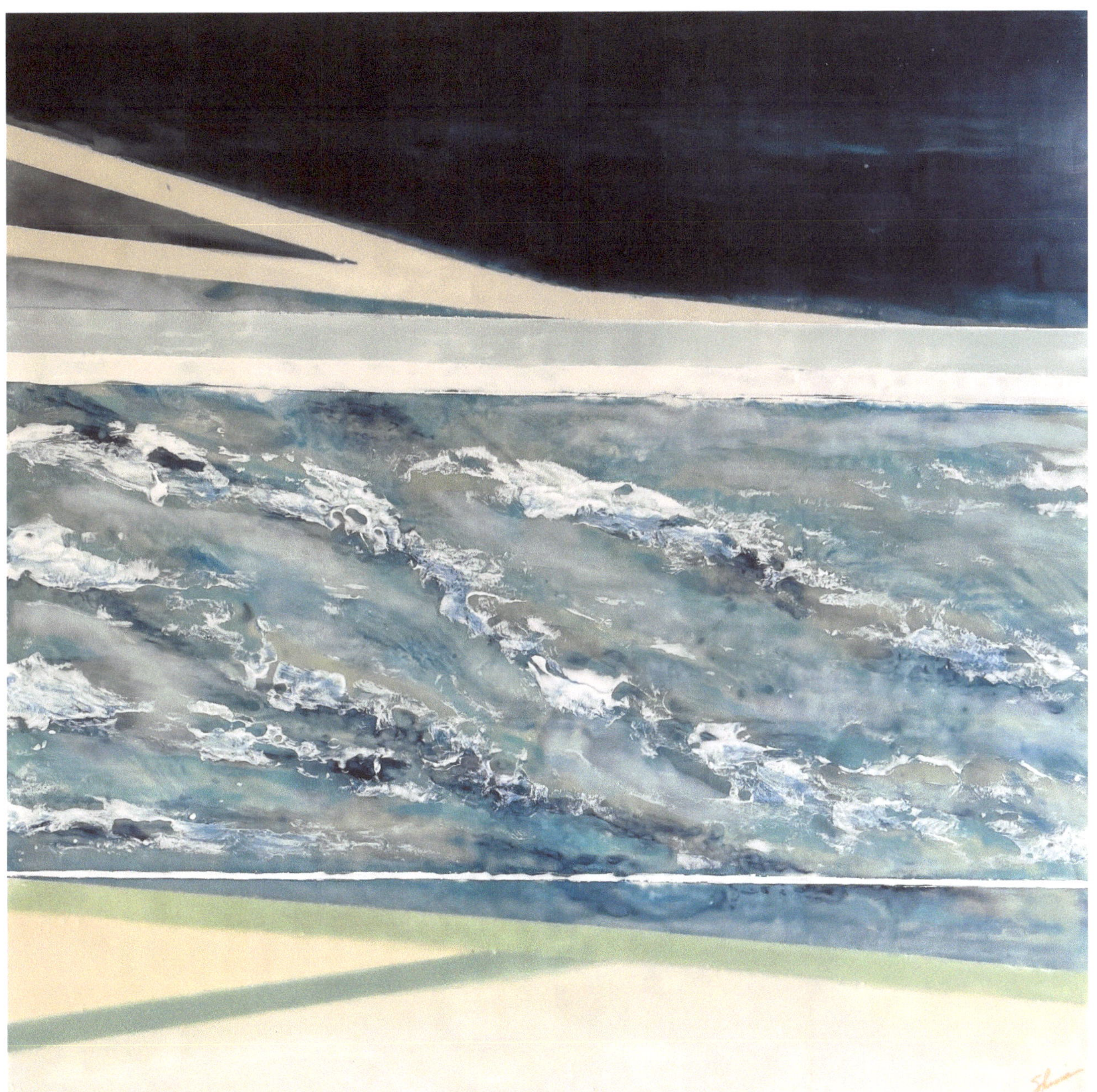

Jeu d'esprit

36 x 36 in

June 2022

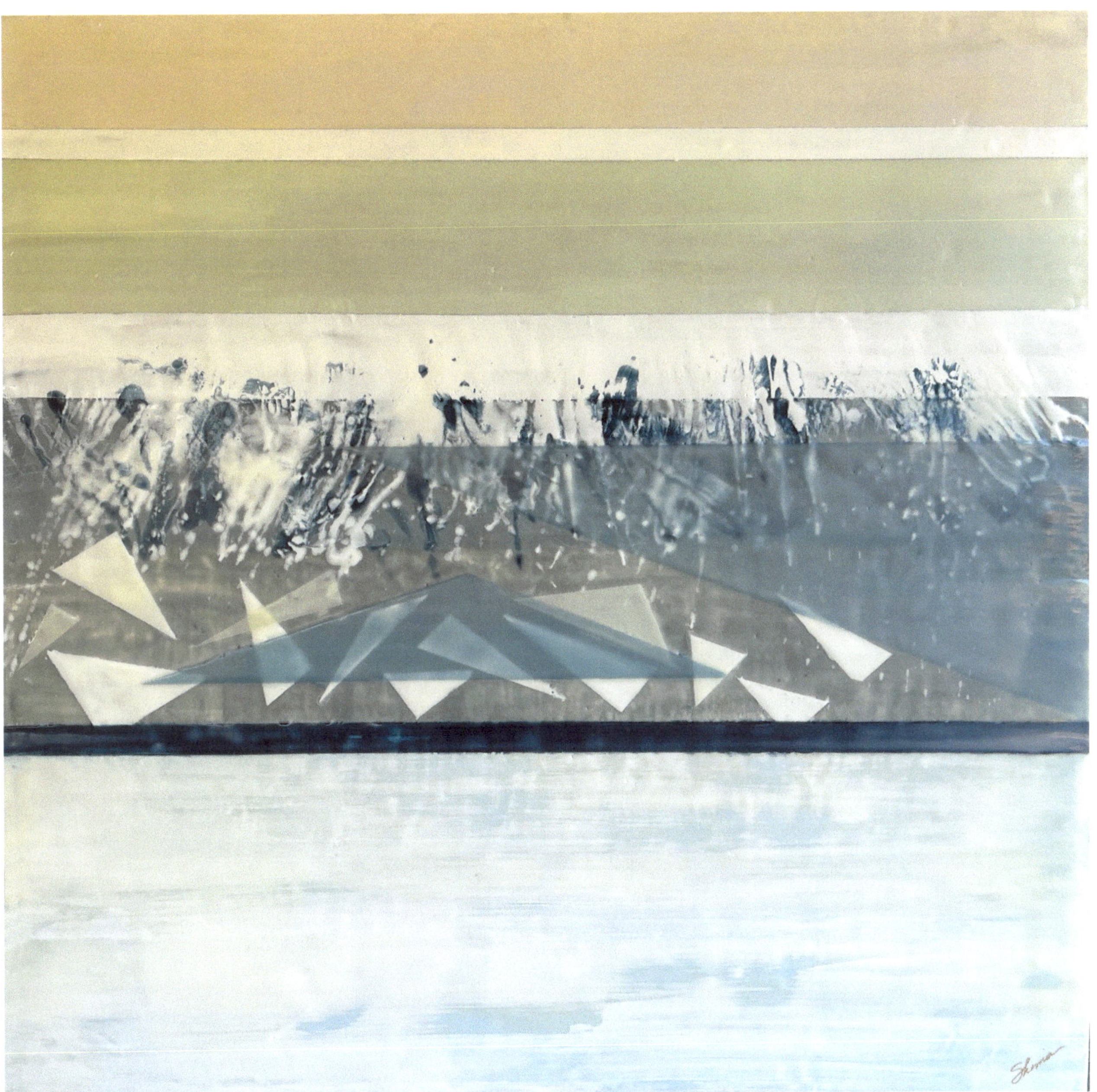

Ley Lines

36 x 36 in

May 2020

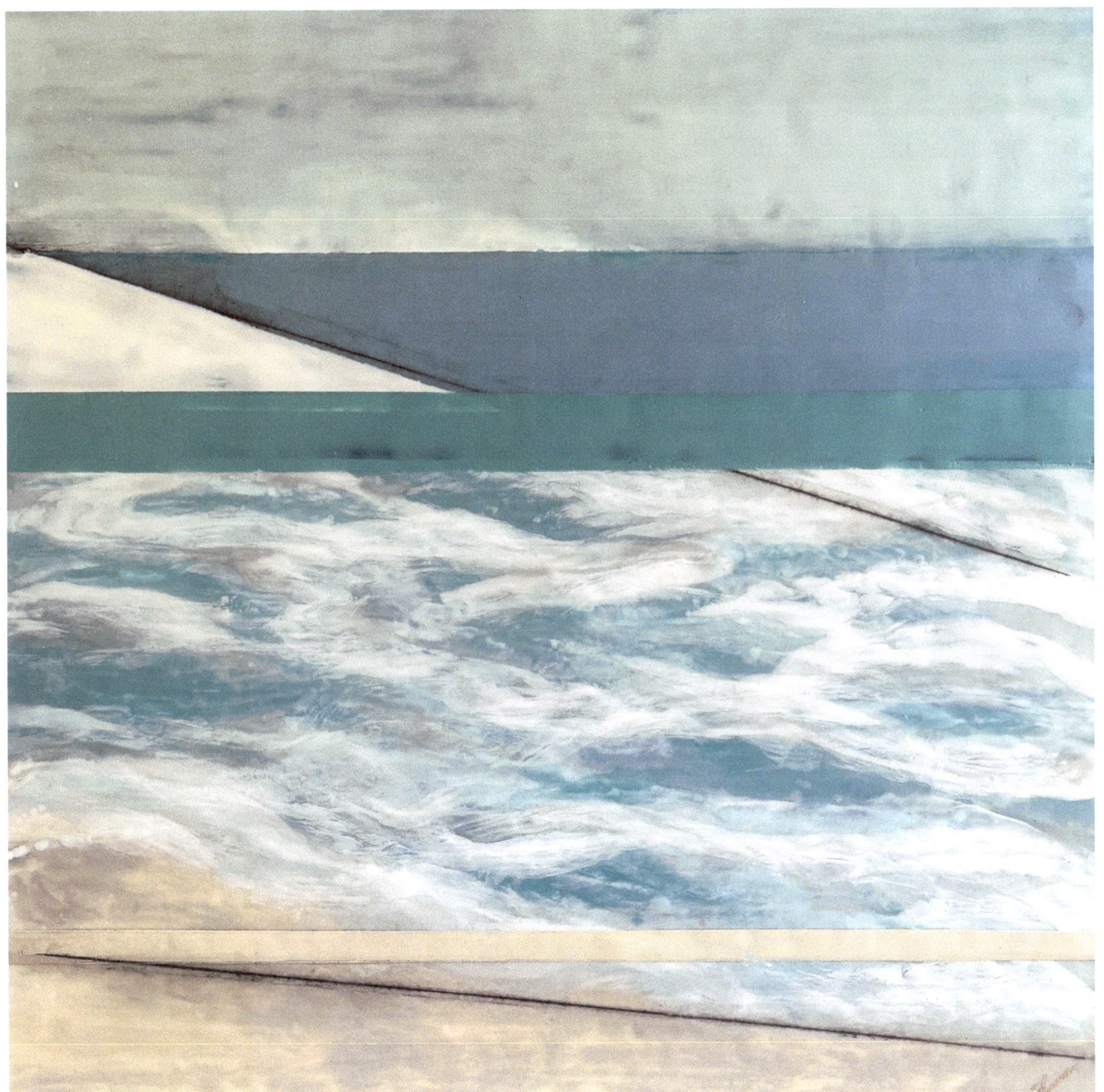

Sea Level 2

36 x 36 in

March 2022

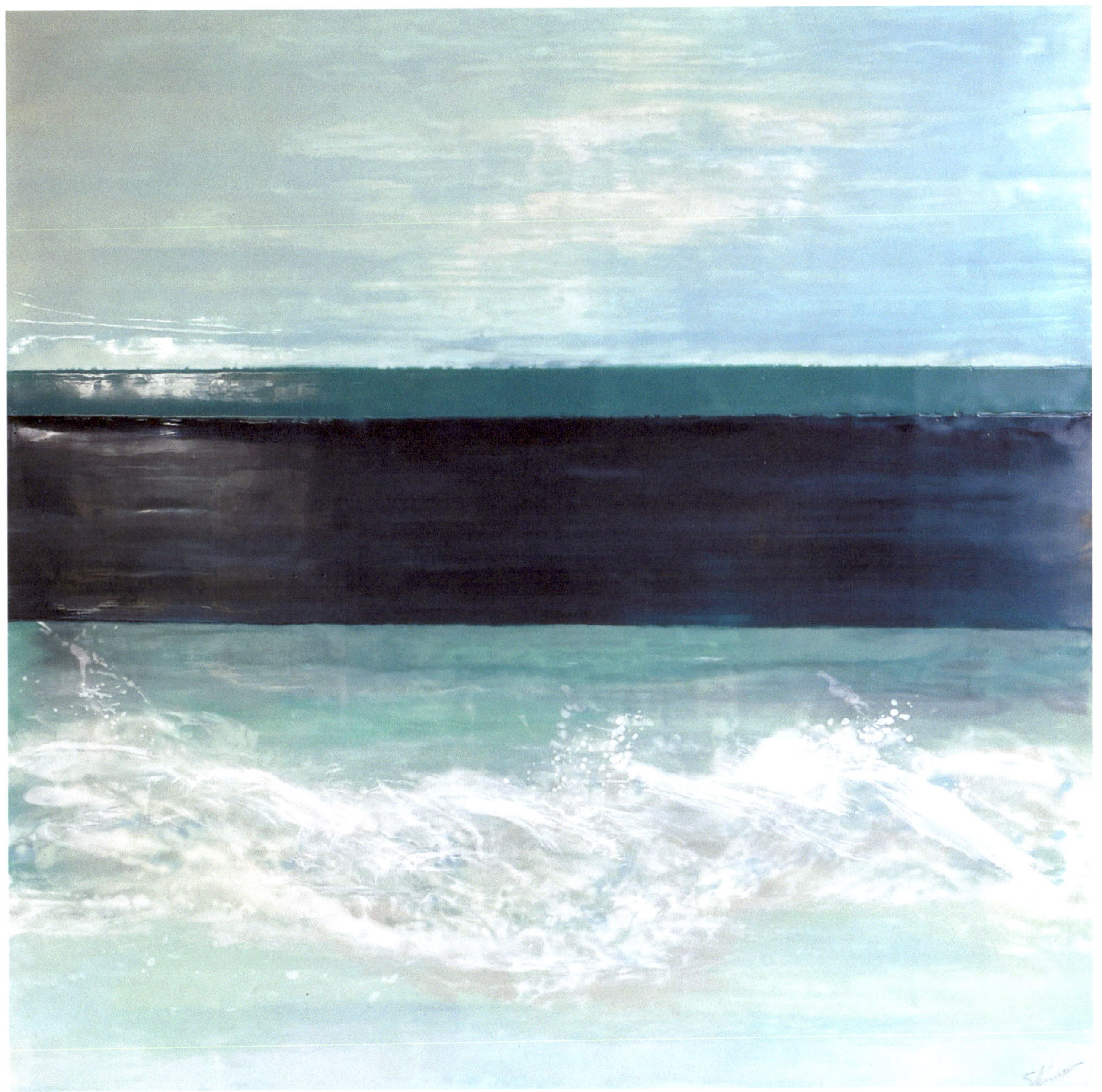

The Narrow Gate

36 x 36 in

May 2022

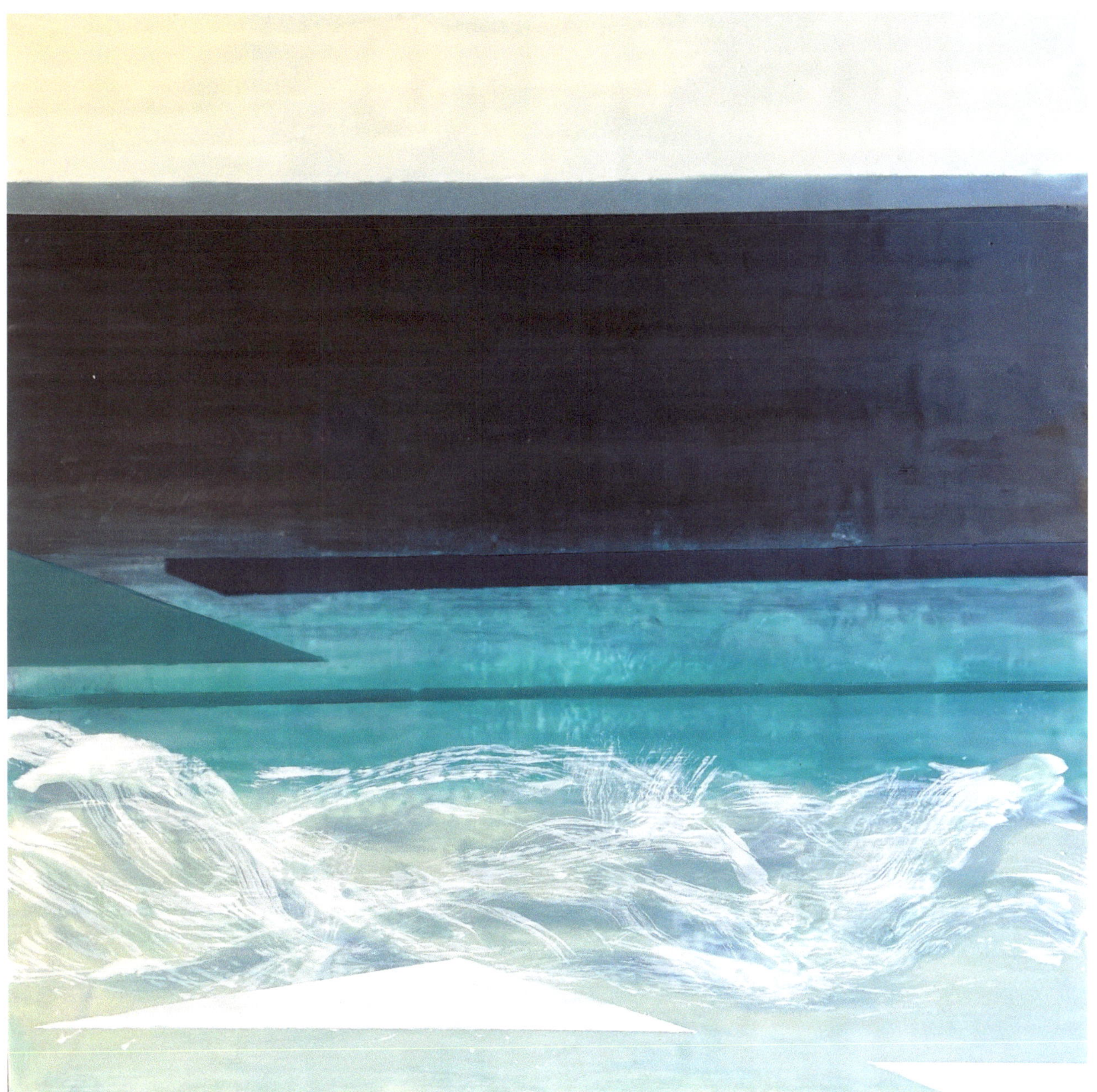

Within Reach

36 x 36 in

June 2022

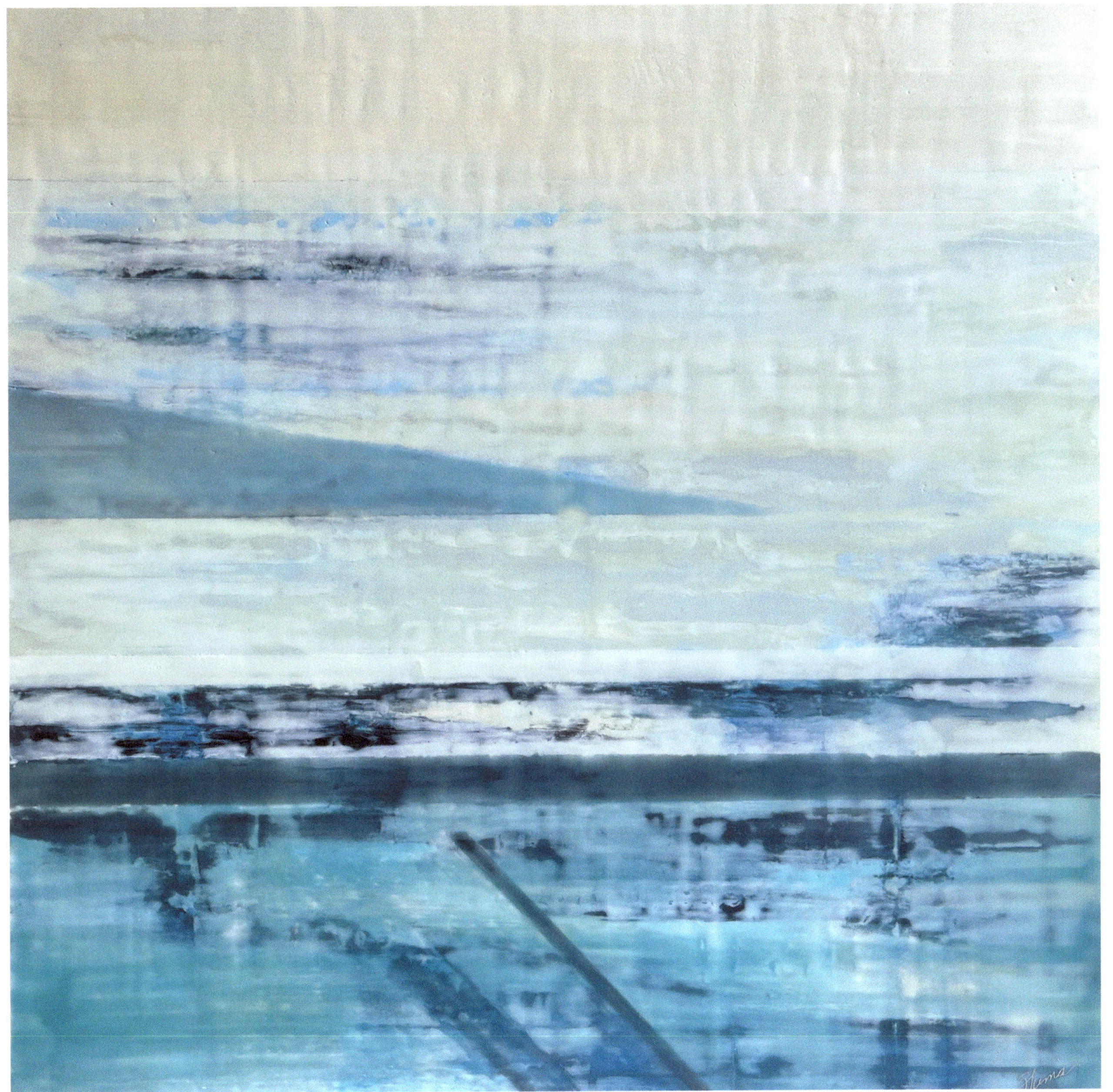

COLLECTION:

LAY OF THE LAND

The meeting place of land and sea.

Earth and water merge.

A transient moment in time.

The fleeting moment where one gives way to the other.

"With each new work I become more assured, less hesitant.

There's no returning to the naivete of my earlier works. Innocence can't be faked.

The timid beauty of hesitation is gone; replaced with assured confidence."

A Brief Slumber

36 x 36 in

January 2022

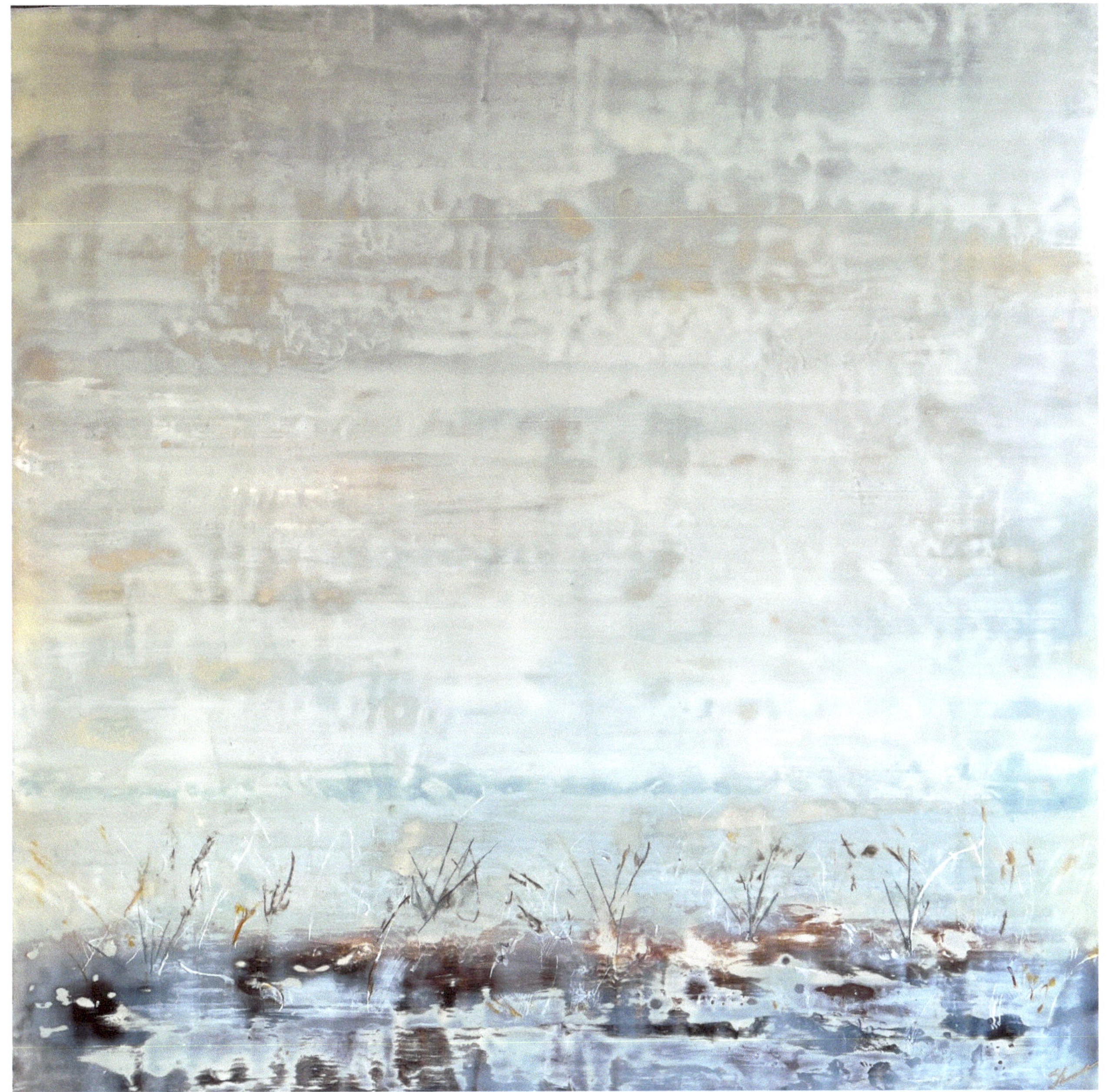

Ascent

36 x 36 in

April 2021

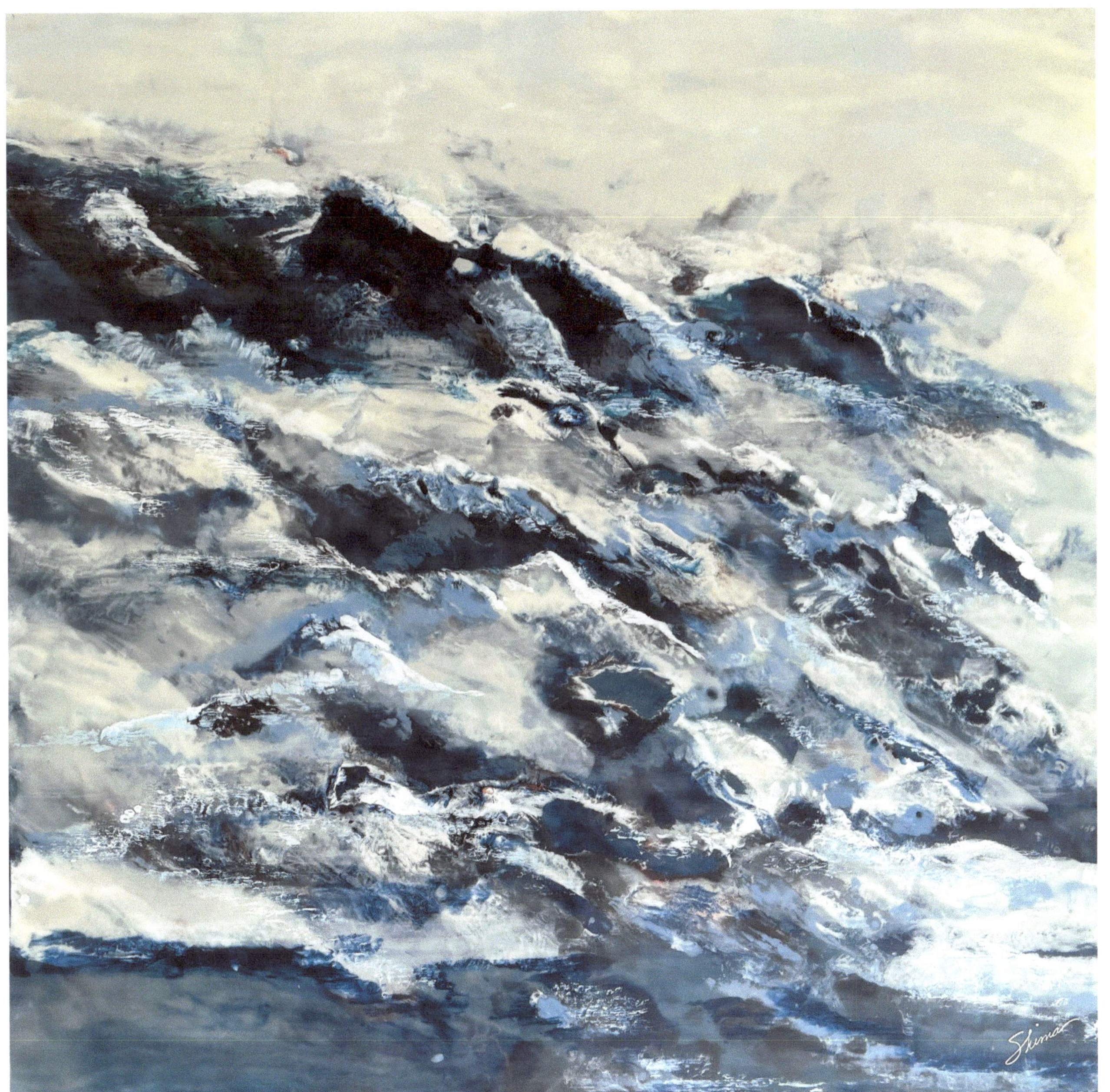

Deepmost I

36 x 36 in

May 2022

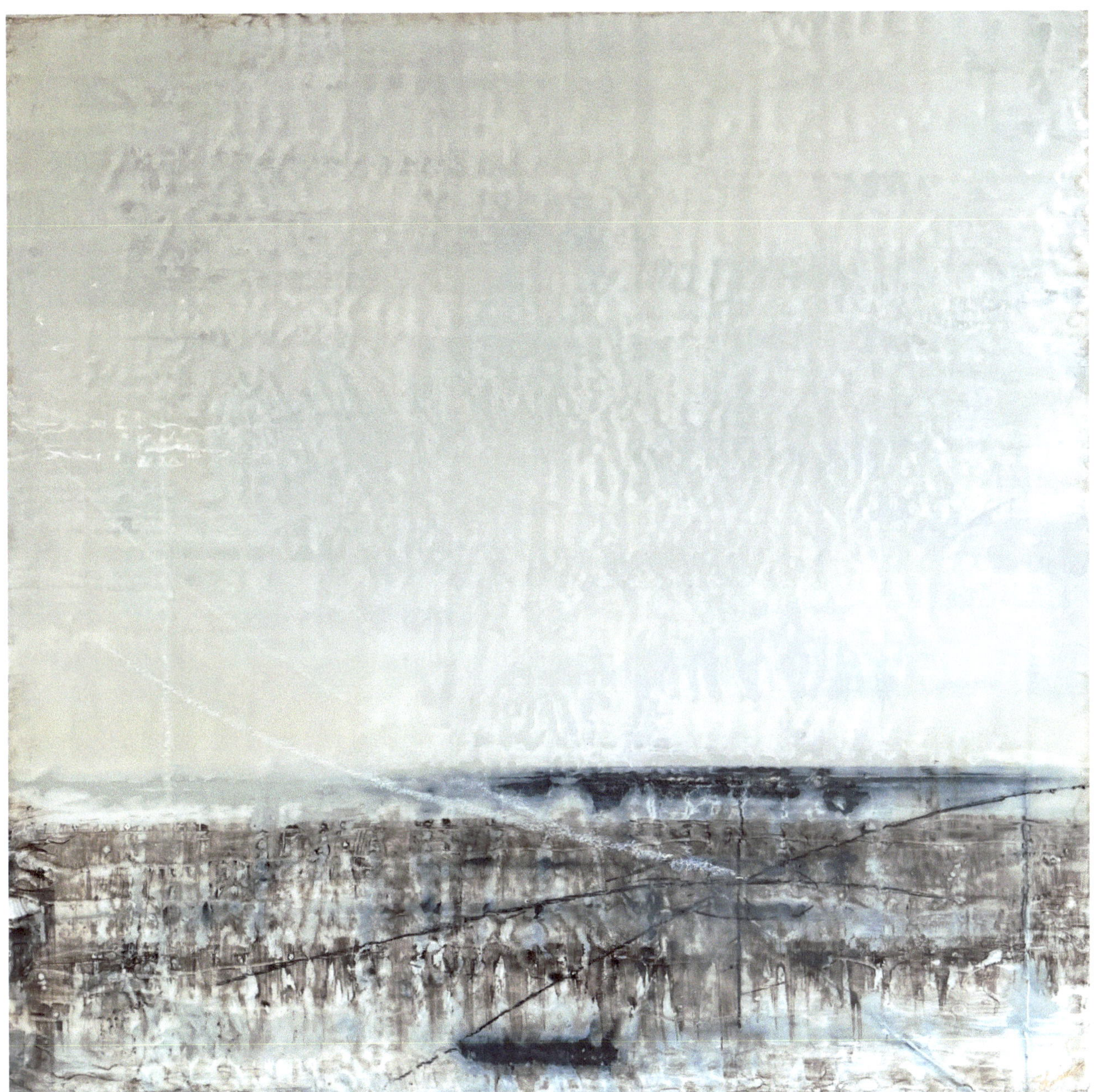

Life Being Lived 2

36 x 36 in

March 2022

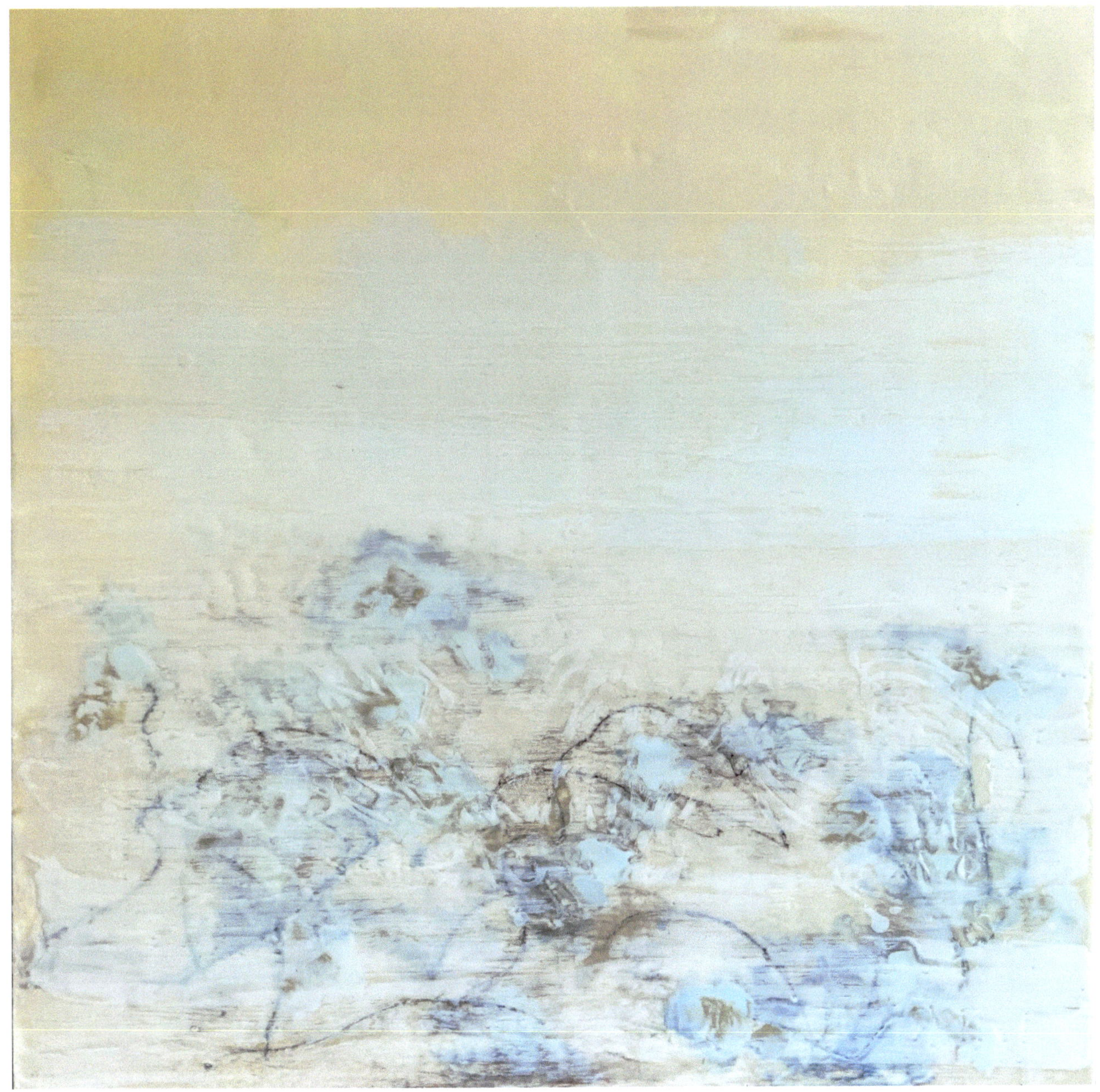

Listless

36 x 36 in

September 2021

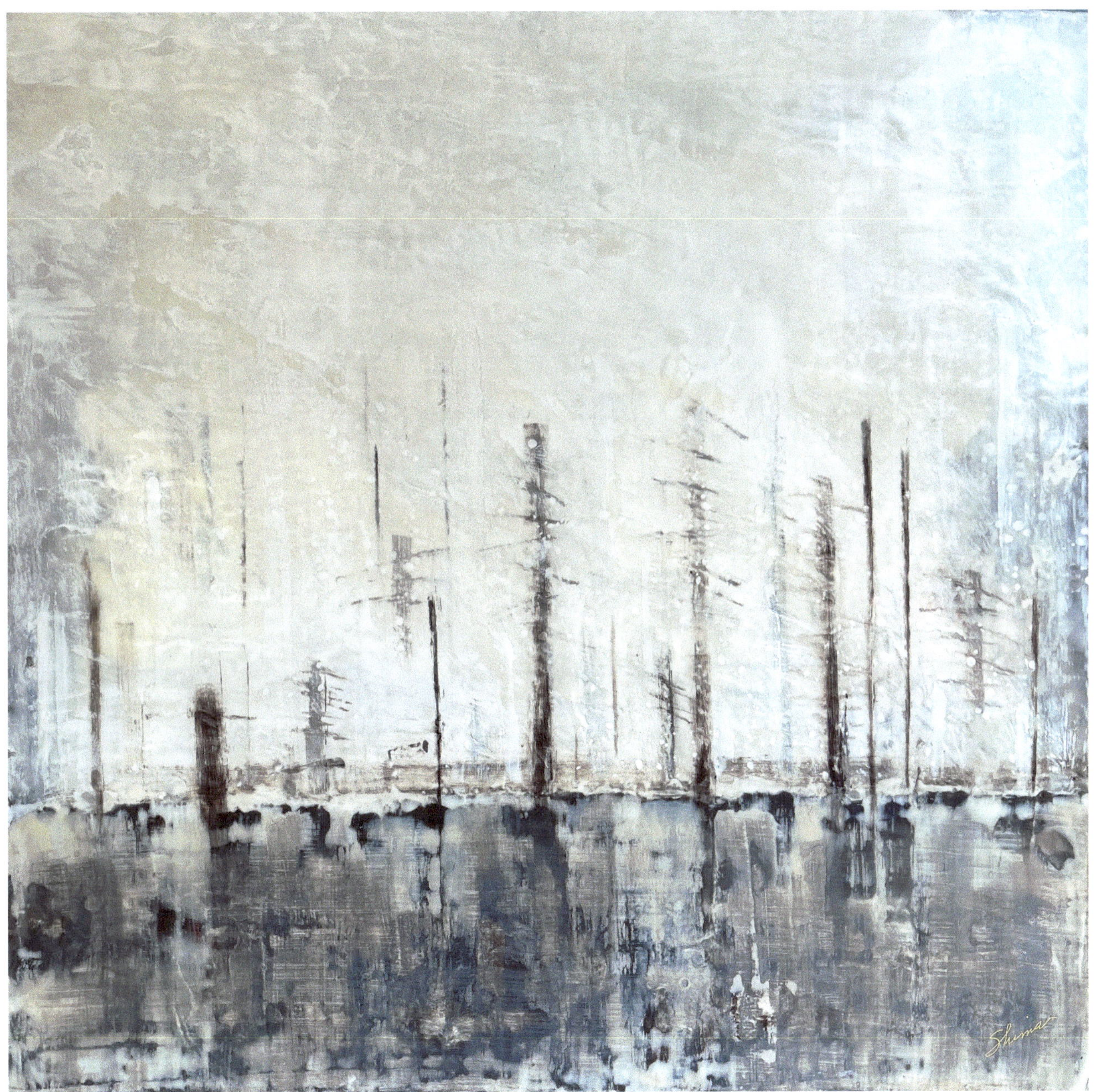

Unbeholdable

36 x 36 in

May 2021

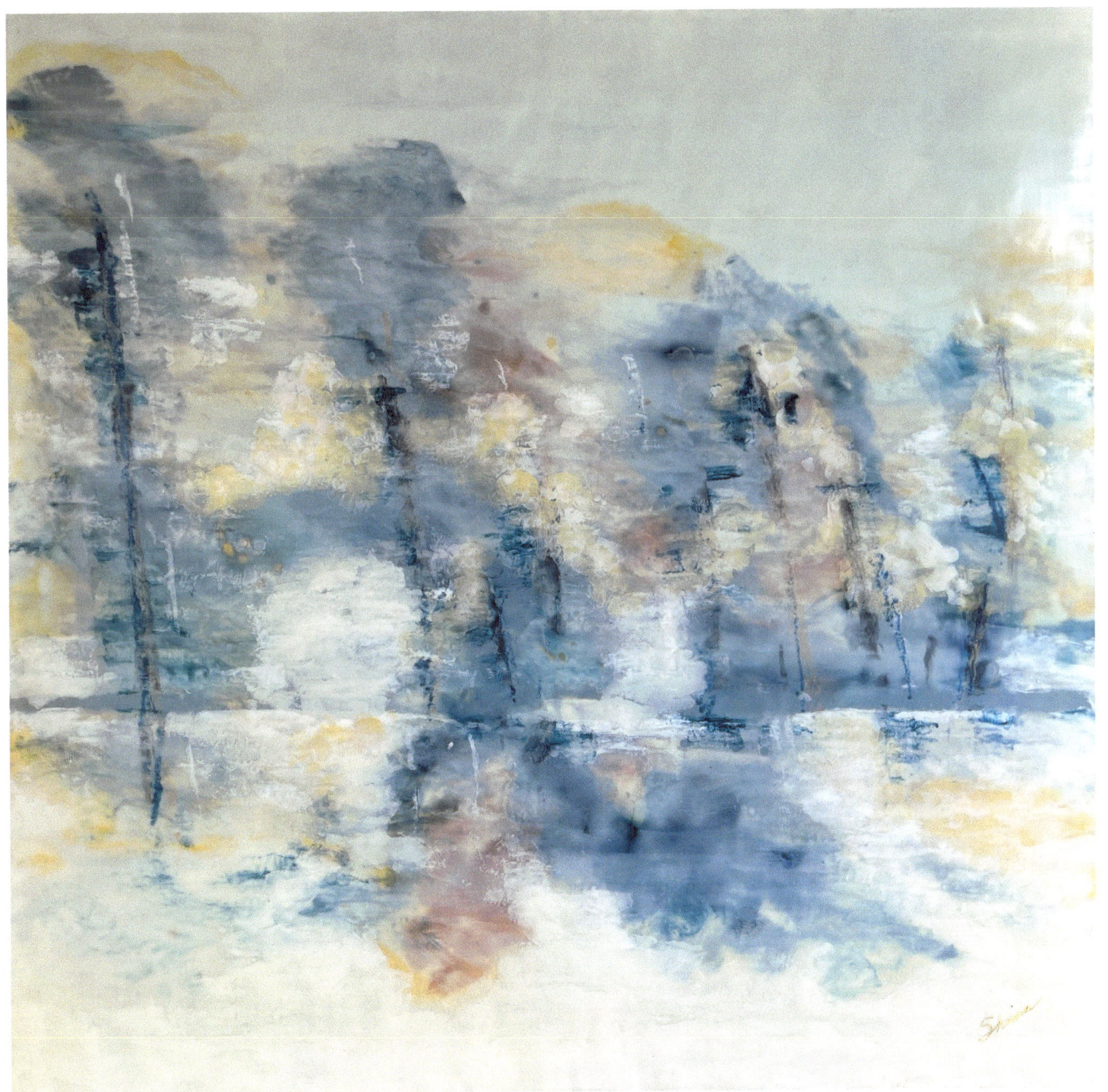

COLLECTION:

URBAN PEACE

A shared space.

A collective conscious.

Individuality and diversity allow for non-conditional acceptance.

"Spiritual mystery is comprised of the unspeakable.

It is hard to put mystical experience into words.

Art transcends our limited vocabulary and enters the realm of mysticism.

It gives us a glimmer of what lies beyond appearance.

The more we comprehend and the deeper we delve, the vaster the mystery becomes."

Confined by Our Own Making

36 x 36 in

June 2022

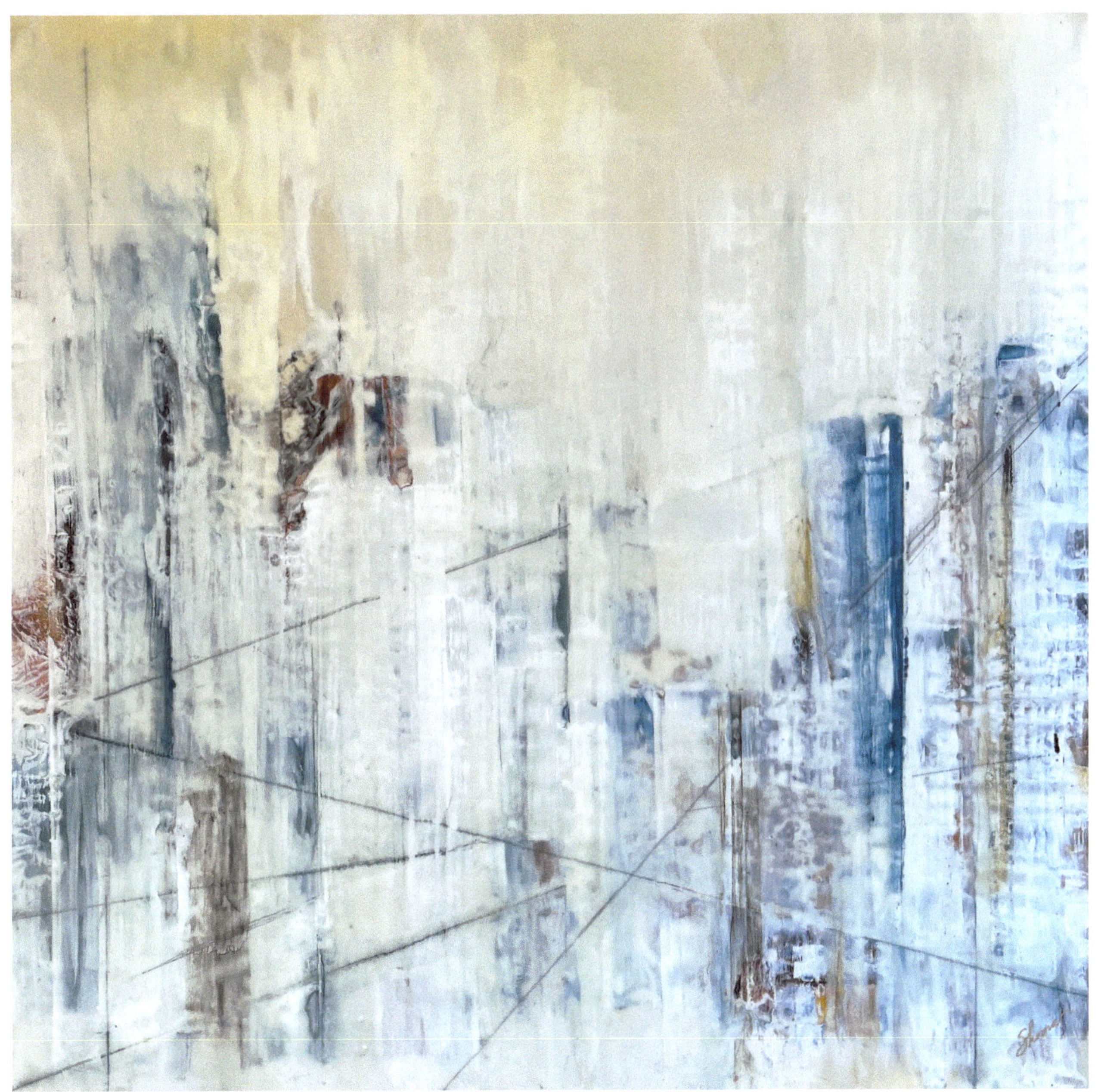

Down Comes the Sky

36 x 36 in

March 2022

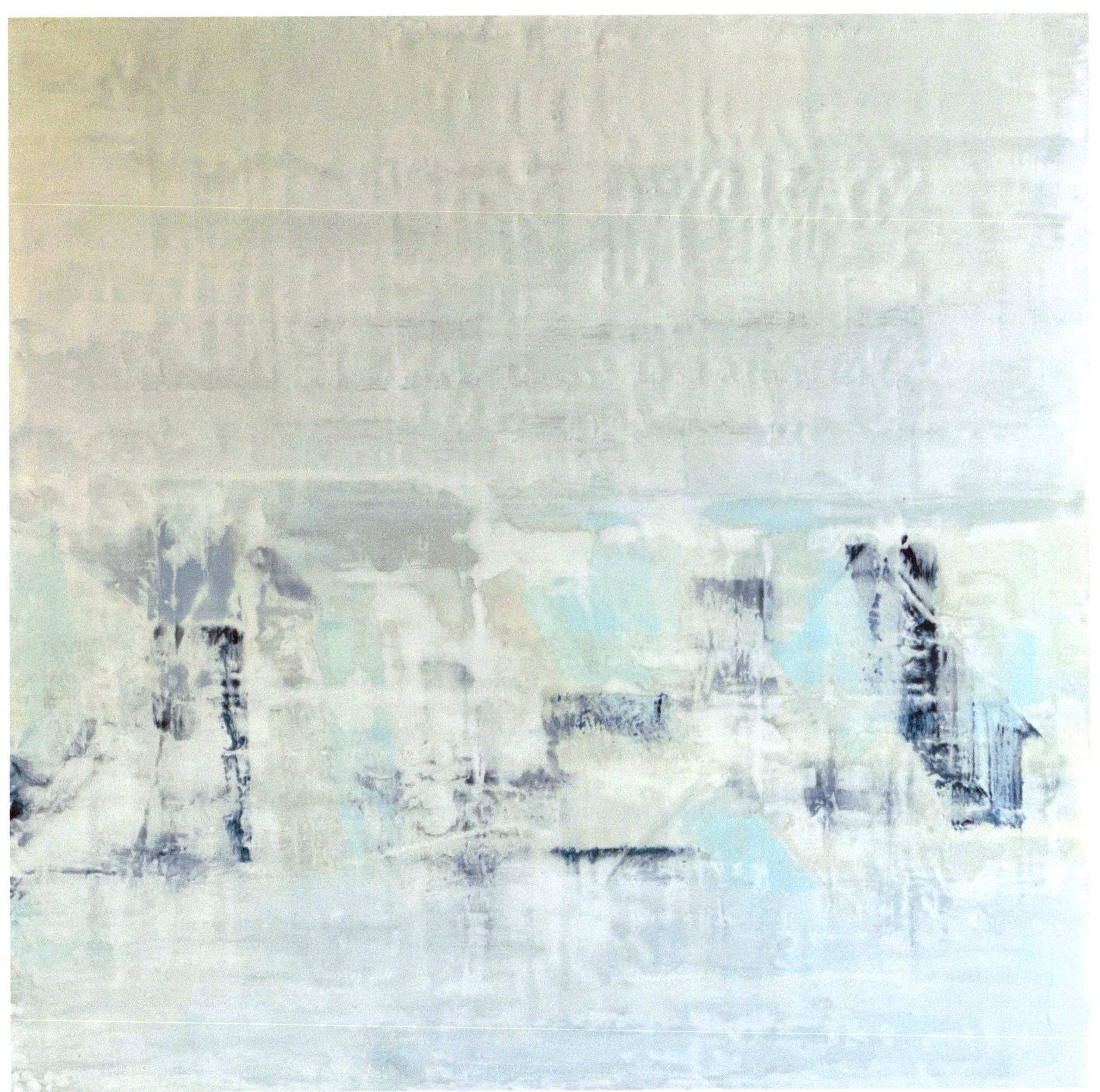

From Every Quarter

36 x 36 in

April 2022

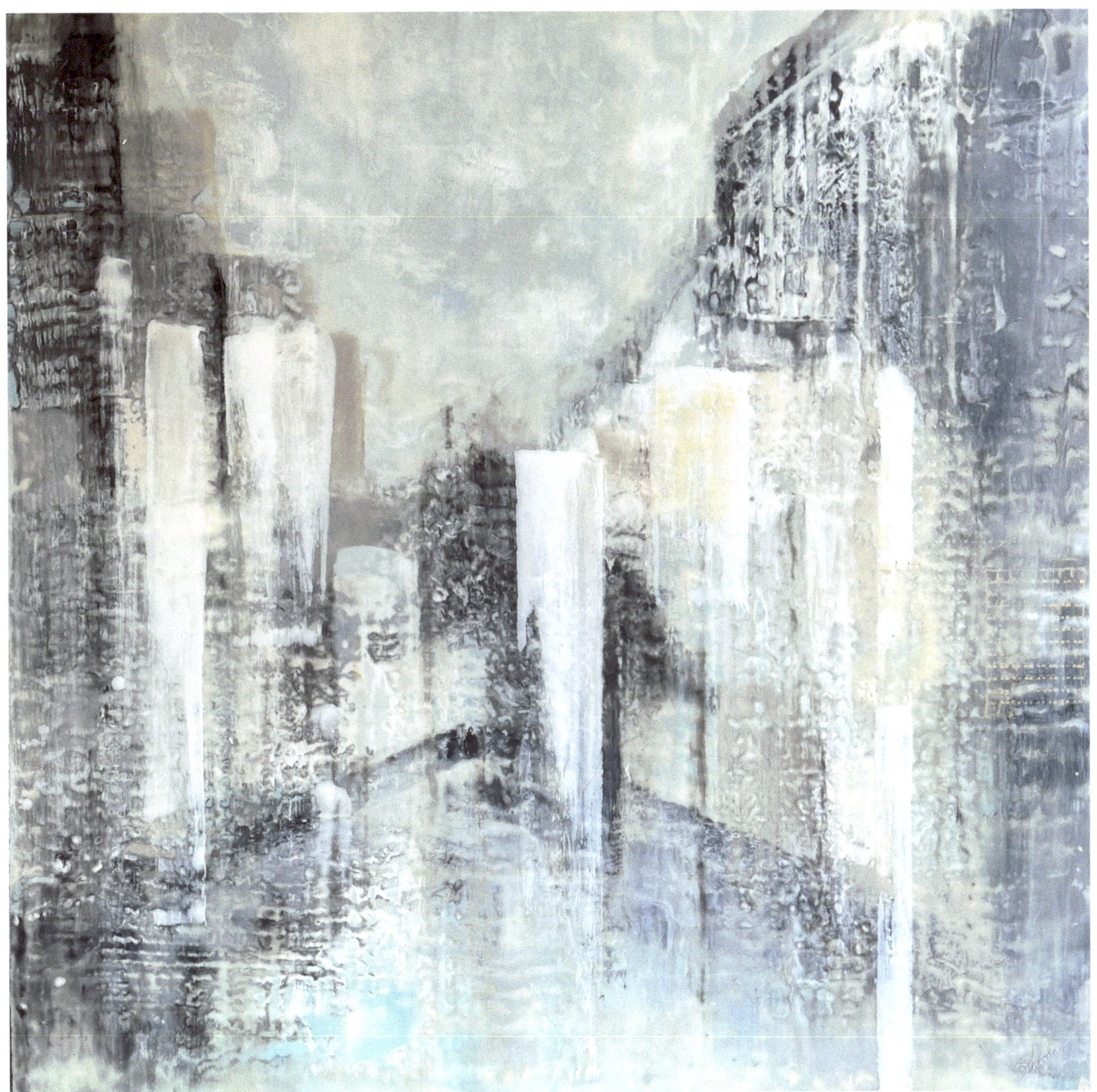

Snow-Still

36 x 36 in

November 2021

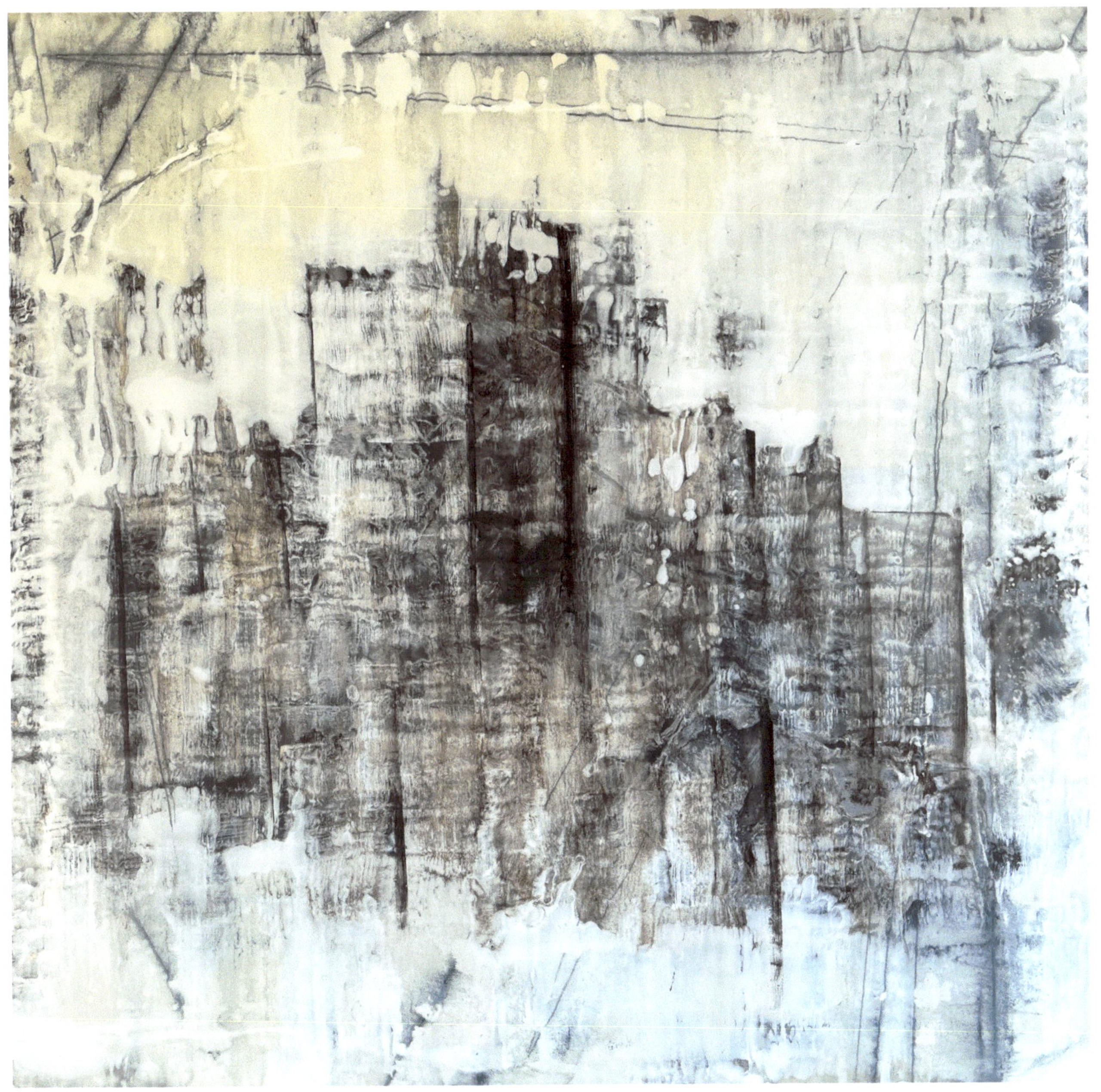

COLLECTION:

WATER IN MOTION

The rhythm and flow of water
conveys a deep sense of peace
even in the most tumultuous sea.

"I am often surprised by the unexpected direction a painting takes.

I must remain uninhibited allowing each painting to reveal its own story."

Effervescence

36 x 36 in

December 2021

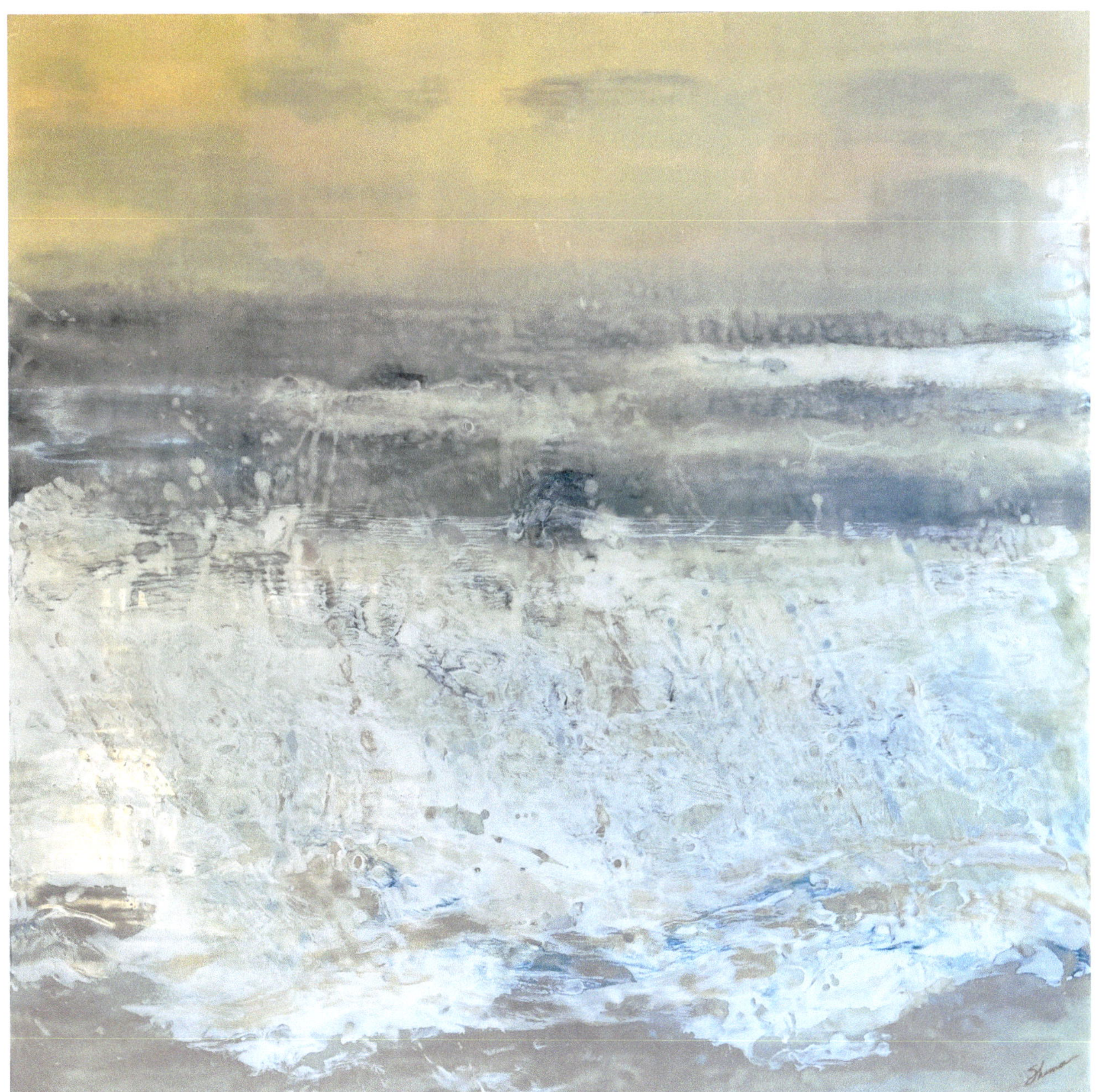

Summoned by the Sea

36 x 36 in

December 2021

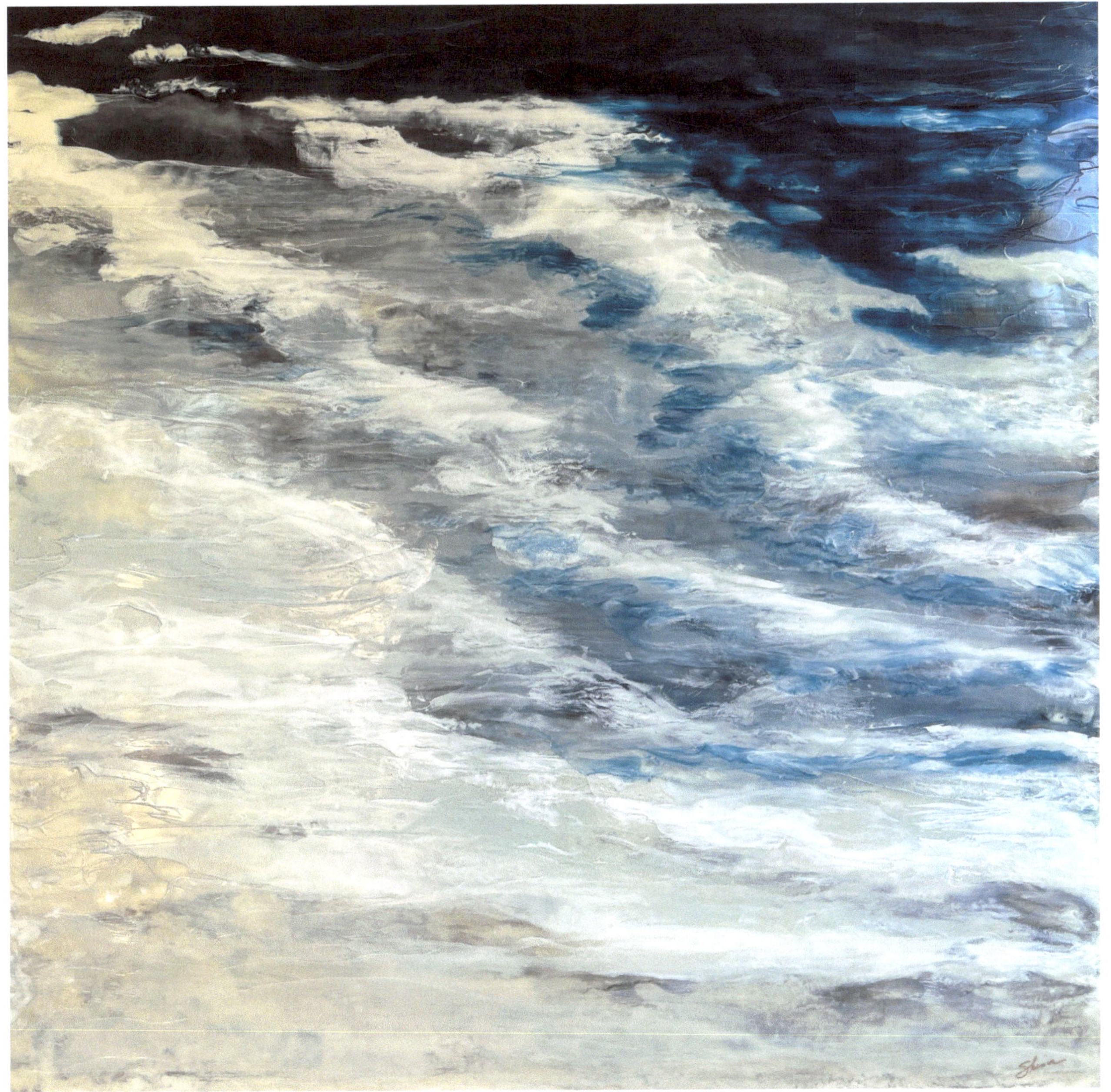

Tears of Jupiter

36 x 36 in

April 2022

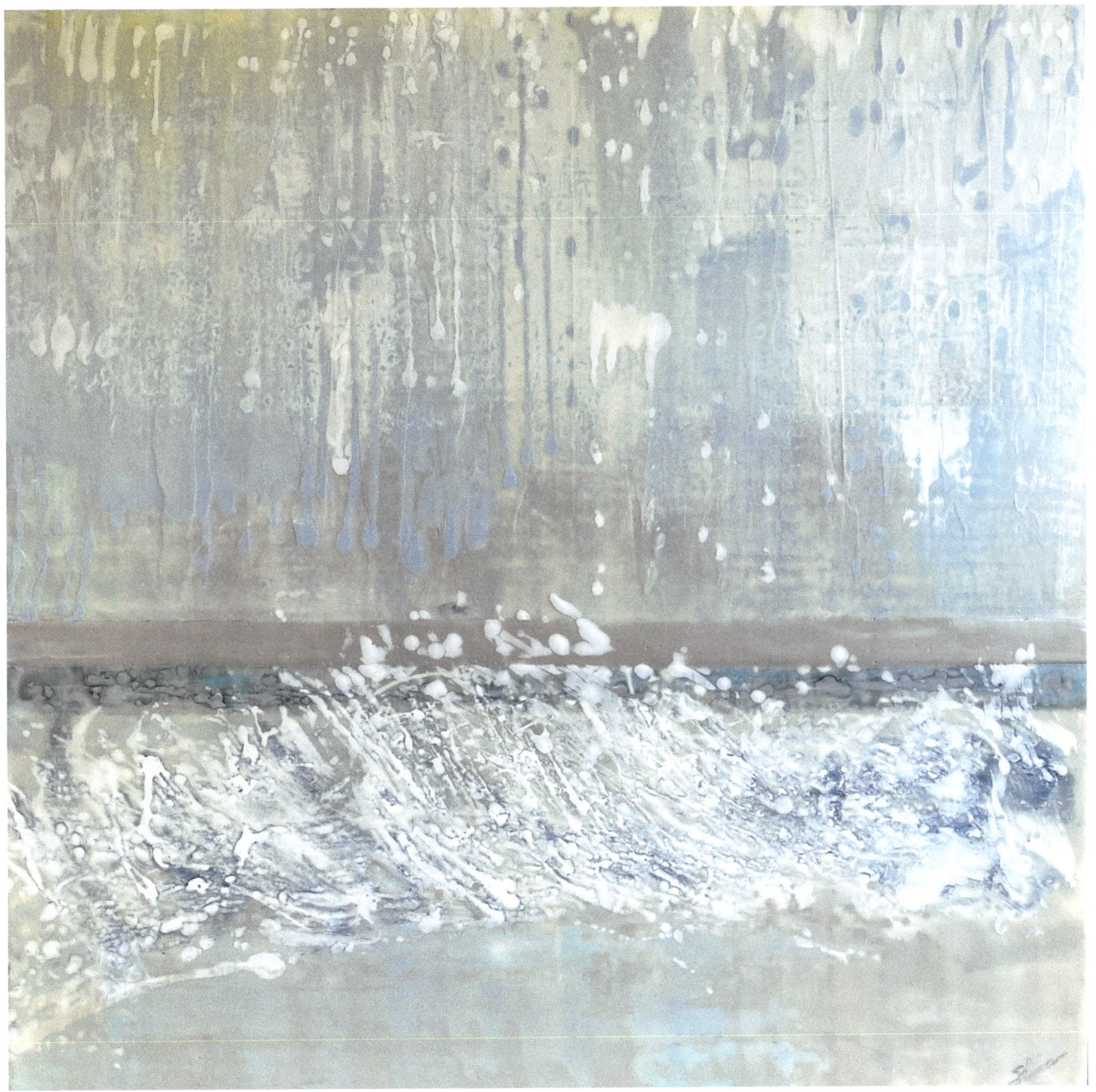

Tears of Laughter 1

36 x 36 in

March 2022

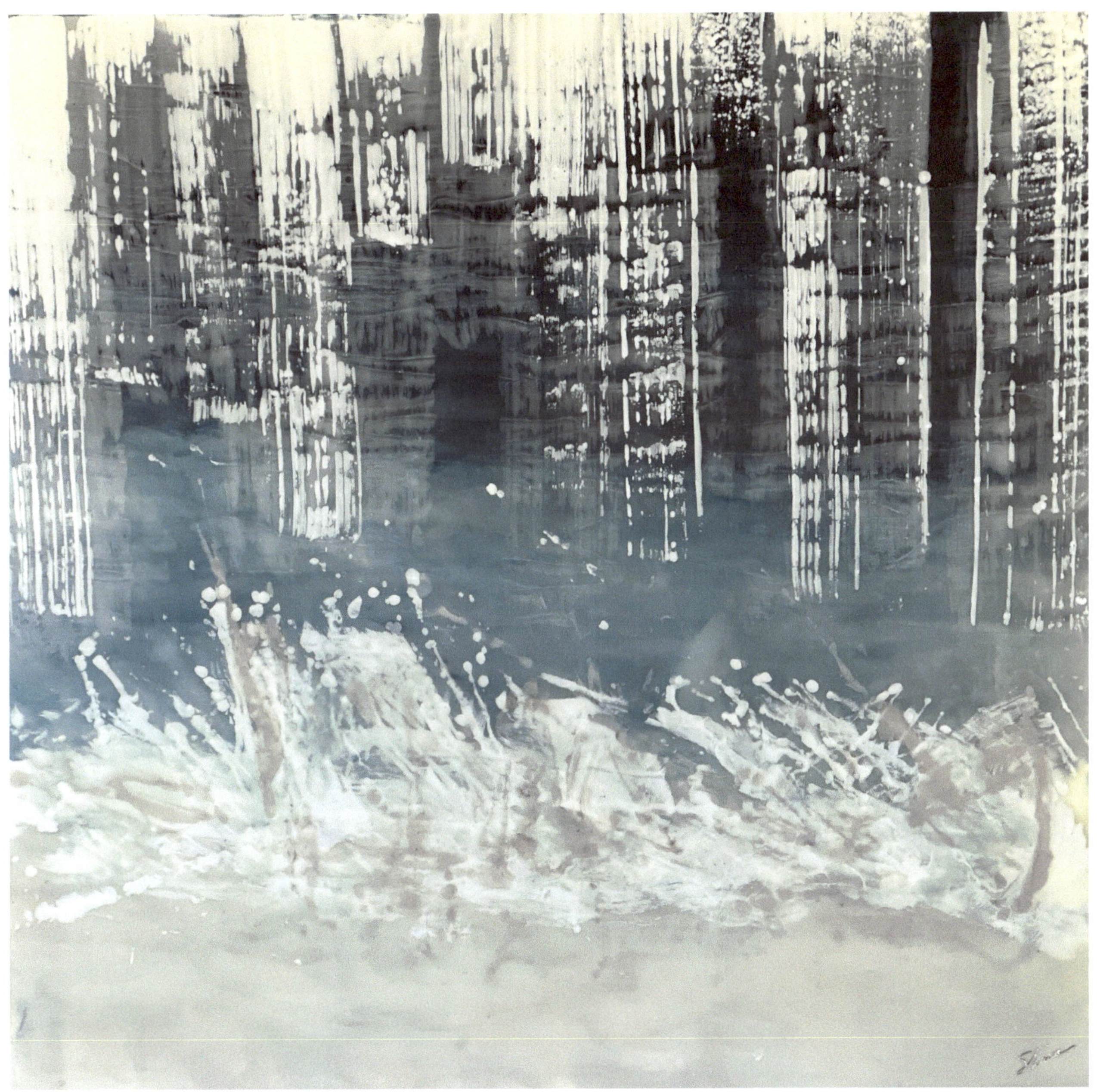

Art is a shared experience.

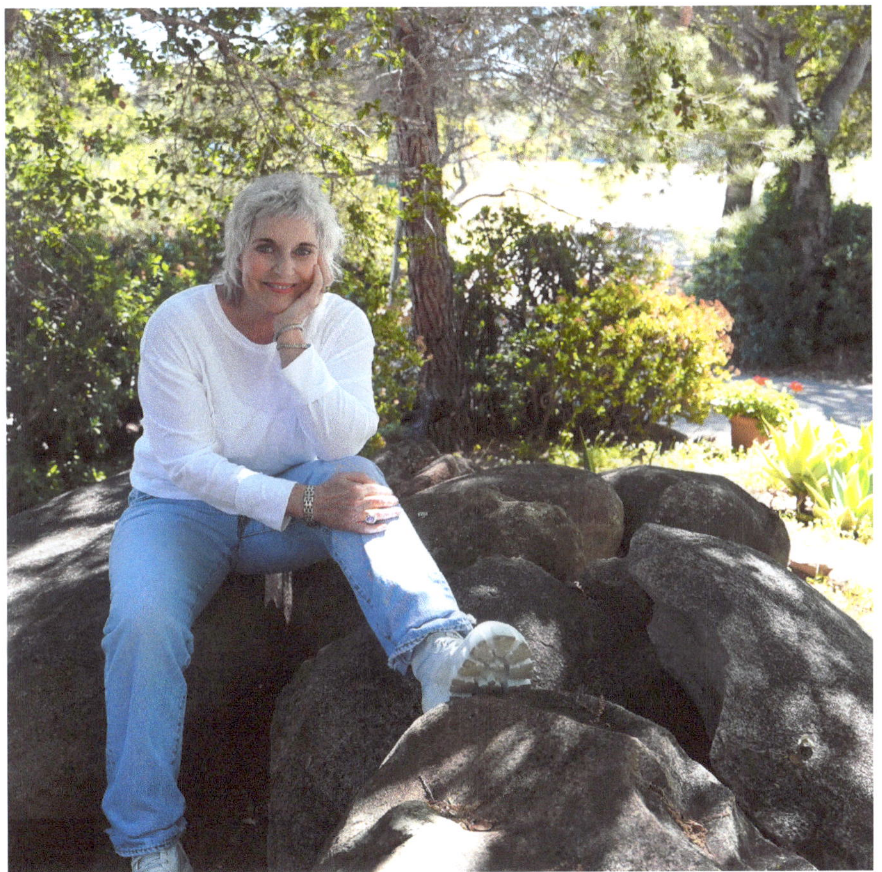

Let's connect.

Shima

Shima@Peacewaters.com
ShimaShanti.com

www.ingramcontent.com/pod-product-compliance
Lightning Source LLC
LaVergne TN
LVHW071631100826
845154LV00008BA/133

9780991548156